The Queen Bees

Also by Stephen Longstreet:

HISTORY

The Wilder Shore (San Francisco)
City on Two Rivers (New York)
War Cries on Horseback (Indian Wars of the West)
Sportin' House (Storyville)
The Real Jazz Old and New
A Treasury of the World's Great Prints
Win or Lose: A Social History of Gambling in America

NOVELS

The Pedlocks
The Beach House
The General
Geisha
Man of Montmartre

PLAY

High Button Shoes

Stephen Longstreet
The Queen Bees
The Women Who Shaped America

The Bobbs-Merrill Company, Inc.
Indianapolis / New York

Library of Congress Cataloging in Publication Data

Longstreet, Stephen, date.
  The queen bees.

  Bibliography: p.
  Includes index.
  1. Women—United States—Biography.
I. Title.
HQ1412.L66   301.41'2'0922   78-11201
0-672-52394-9

iv

To my granddaughter Stacy Robin
showing signs at an early age
of becoming a Queen Bee

Contents

Introduction

I recall a packet of letters and photographs from my grandmother's days which evoked frequent comments about how forgotten were the women of her youth who did so much—"the Queen Bees," she called them—those women who laid the foundation for the present ferment for women's rights.

As I handled her collection of old photographs, I realized that indeed these women have for the most part been forgotten. Those who are remembered have become legends and myths. Ahead of their time, they initiated the trends that played such an important part in releasing women from bondage to home, children and bed. Their efforts greatly changed the color of our life, its fashions, and its moods.

For this book I have selected women from various stratifications of our past, choosing here and there from among the highs and lows of our culture, seeking a true cross section of individuals that would represent the thousands who strived, who were abused or mocked, or who sat high in the pecking order under hereditary tiaras. They were chosen, regardless of their backgrounds, to fit the pattern. Some were martyrs, some fools and snobs; a few were fanatics. There is even a sexual adventuress or two, next to the avant-gardists, lesbians and ordinary housewives.

This book is a rediscovery of the matriarchs and the female reformers who altered American social and legal standards—women who followed Amelia Bloomer; who cried out for the ballot box, sexual equality, and the opportunity for equal rights to jobs in a man's world; who supported Carrie Nation and Margaret Sanger.

Some of these women and their families have, for two hundred years, been considered by others (and themselves) as SOCIETY. At face value these women's lives appear to be chronicles of scandals, of wild living, huge parties and wasted fortunes. Referring to them as "the idle rich" or with a mocking "Mrs. Astor's Pet Horse," however, only reiterates outworn and undesirable epithets. I try to show their largely unnoticed contributions to the American scene.

Such women, who in many cases headed dynasties, brought to American culture a great civilizing force, beginning with the teaching of manners and social graces and the introduction into rough native cooking of ideas from better cuisines. As fashion-setters, they attracted attention with their modish imported attire, and soon the shopgirl and the housewife began to dress with greater style. In addition to leading the fight in support of women's rights, they introduced, among other things, bathrooms and daily hygiene. They brought the first Impressionist paintings into the country—while the men were still collecting "Old Masters," false Corots and Salon pinups by second-rate artists.

While the men made the money, the women made a much-envied society; they created fêtes, balls and parties from Fifth Avenue to Newport and from Palm Beach to Santa Barbara. Their efforts had a solid theme: Theirs were the voices of society, and they went beyond the simple snobbery of the "400." These women gloried in their own tastes, which, although sometimes bad, were often civilizing.

Trekking east to enter society, the wives of rich miners, railroad kings, and the first oil barons transformed social habits. The glory of a social set and its table manners could be charted as its influence moved on to Chicago, San Francisco and interior points like St. Louis, Cleveland and St. Paul, creating settings which in turn revealed new standards in the matter of *who* lived on the right side of the silver spoons and the damask tablecloths.

Irish and Jewish women were also Queen Bees of their hives. No more closely knit society existed (and perhaps exists today) than their proud, successful second and third generations. The great Irish families—the McDonalds, the Butlers, the Kellys (Princess Grace),

The Kennedys, the Buckleys—all produced women who dominated generations as they steered their families from the shanty to political king-making.

The Jews developed into clans like the DePools, Cardozas, Kahns; the Lehmans, Strausses, Warbergs and Guggenheims—all ruled by women. There were the breakaways into the ranks of the goyem— the Belmonts, the Goldwassers (Goldwater), the Dillons, and the Mark Clarks. The Russian Jews produced, among others, the social stars: the Paleys, Baruchs and Sarnoffs—in a society dominated by that stereotype, the Jewish mother.

I have brought forward some of the remarkable women of the Southwest who rose to social and political power in Texas, California and other states. Some were not content just to accumulate fortunes in cattle, oil, publishing and politics and then become satisfied prey of Neiman-Marcus or Gucci. There were Murchisons, Mavericks, Hunts, King Ranch stock, and those Gulf Coast women who helped to establish a new style in tropical living. Legend is filled with undocumented dramas about a society of Barbary Coast gals married to 49ers. Living in Pasadena, Santa Barbara, Carmel, Palm Springs and San Francisco today are families whose women helped produce the modern West Coast. Dorothy "Buffy" Chandler, who helped rule the Los Angeles *Times* empire and hassled the Culture Center ($60 million) to completion, is only one example.

I do want to make clear what this book is *not*. It is not a collection of biographies of well-known women, nor is it a clinical study of the American female. Rather, I have described a carefully selected group of women who helped civilize much of this nation. Some set new social patterns; others worked in new art forms; some attracted attention in socially unacceptable ways. Those I have chosen are merely representative; dozens of others could have been cited. This selection includes certain figures who may have lacked public virtue or even a clearly defined purpose. Not all were "good" women in the accepted moralities of the past. Yet both knowingly and unknowingly all did effect change, not just in the women's world, but on the national scene. If some were not always queens and others not bees buzzing steadily at their tasks, they all were in some way remarkable.

I have investigated original texts, letters, journals and old newspapers and magazines and have dug into many books in and out of print. Over the course of the many years I spent planning this book, I conducted detailed interviews with women in many fields, and I sought the opinions of many groups. Much of the information I gleaned is distilled and condensed in the text.

In these changing times I was not surprised to discover at a meeting of the WOMEN FOR organization (on the West Coast) some graffiti, still damp on a wall, reading: NATURE MEANT WOMAN TO BE HER MASTERPIECE.

Stephen Longstreet
Miradero Road
California
1978

The Queen Bees

The bee is more honored than other animals
not because she labors,
but because she labors for others.

Anonymous

Prologue
Mrs. Trollope's Visit

In the fall of 1827, Frances Trollope, a refined, intelligent English-woman, embarked from London to face the American wilderness in Cincinnati, Ohio. Here she planned to establish a sort of department store, The Bazaar. She was in a quandary about going into trade, never having had any experience in running a store, and the idea must have embarrassed her; perhaps she hoped that the people back home would not know what enterprise she hoped to found in America in order to mend the family fortunes.

She was desperate and determined. Her husband, Thomas Anthony, was a scholar long past his student days, a failure who devoted his time to writing some large, never-to-be-finished tome on an obscure subject. Their hopes of inheriting a fortune had faded with the remarriage of a rich old uncle and the birth of his heir. The Trollopes had heard of the New World, of the drive of aggressive Americans, and of fortunes to be made there in furs, in merchandising and textiles, and in crops of cotton, corn and tobacco. Mrs. Trollope went first, taking the three of her five children most fit to travel. Her son Anthony Trollope, the future great Victorian novelist, was twelve at the time; he remained in school in England.

The plan was for them to land at New Orleans; stay awhile with an English friend at a raw settlement, Nashoba; then go up the wide Mississippi and the Ohio to the thriving city of Cincinnati. Here the tasteful imports of the Trollopes would, it was hoped, make them merchants of great and good fortune.

Frances Trollope was no lowly emigrant with packs and rope-tied parcels. The party, besides son Henry, included daughters Emily and Cecilia, a proper manservant, and a royalist fugitive from France,

Frances Trollope, author of the revealing book The Domestic Habits of the Americans.

Auguste Hervieu. He was thirty-three, an artist of some talent, prepared to make his fortune by painting portraits of well-off citizens along the Mississippi. Was he Frances Trollope's lover? Victorian decorum draws the shades here.

Mrs. Trollope had no intention at that time of writing a book, but, having an acute sensibility and a keen eye for detail and for what was mannerly and proper, she made many notes.

The habits of native Americans appalled her. She noted, for

instance, the vile habit of chewing tobacco, commenting that "the spitting was incessant." On the drinking of raw spirits she commented:

> *Ardent spirits, though lamentably cheap, still cost something, and the use of them among the men, with more or less of discretion, according to the character, is universal. Tobacco also grows at their doors, and is not taxed; yet this too costs something, and the air of heaven is not in more general use among the men of America than chewing tobacco. I am not now pointing out the evils of dram-drinking, but it is evident that where this practice prevails universally, and often to the most frightful excess, the consequences must be, that the money spent to obtain the dram is less than the money lost by the time consumed in drinking it. Long, disabling, and expensive fits of sickness are incontestably more frequent in every part of America than in England, and the sufferers have no aid to look to, but what they have saved, or what they may be enabled to sell. I have never seen misery exceed what I have witnessed in an American cottage where disease has entered.*

Her comment on American women of all classes is a fitting prelude to this book. Her picture of woman's condition is one of the few contemporary descriptions we have from a female point of view.

> *If the condition of the labourer be not superior to that of the English peasant, that of his wife and daughters is incomparably worse. It is they who are indeed the slaves of the soil. One has but to look at the wife of an American cottager, and ask her age, to be convinced that the life she leads is one of hardship and privation and labour. It is rare to see a woman in this station who has reached the age of thirty, without losing every trace of youth and beauty. You continually see women with infants on their knee that you feel sure are their grand-children, till some convincing proof to the contrary is displayed. Even the young girls, though often with lovely features, look pale, thin and haggard. I do not remember to have seen any single instance among the poor, a specimen of the plump, rosy, laughing physiognomy so common among our cottage girls. The horror of domestic service, which the reality of slavery and the*

fable of equality have generated, excludes the young women from that
sure and most comfortable resource . . . and the consequence is that with
a most irreverent freedom of manner to the parents, the daughters are, to
the full extent of the word, domestic slaves. This condition, which no
periodical merry-making, no village fête, ever occurs to cheer, is only
changed for the still sadder burdens of a teeming wife. They marry very
young; in fact in no rank of life do you meet with young women in that
delightful period of existence between childhood and marriage, wherein,
if only tolerably well spent, so much useful information is gained, and
the character takes on a sufficient degree of firmness to support with
dignity the more important parts of wife and mother. The slender,
childish thing, without vigour of mind or body, is made to stem a sea of
troubles that dims her young eye and makes her cheek grow pale, even
before nature has given it the last beautiful finish of the full-grown
woman.

When she reached Cincinnati after a hard journey, Mrs. Trollope's
first impression was that of a crude, busy place. Here she felt the
Trollopes could become comfortably well off, even rich, for in
twenty-five years this muddy village had become a town of 20,000
inhabitants, doing several million dollars' worth of business a year.
She noted that it dealt—with no disparagement or shame—in
whiskey (an easy way to ship corn crops in kegs), as well as in flour
and salt pork. Pigs were everyplace. Great steam riverboats—many
of which blew up—were built there, and there were iron foundries,
printing establishments, sugar refineries.

Mrs. Trollope took part in whatever artistic project the town
provided, while the French artist painted scenery and portraits and
made sardonic drawings in the style of a minor Hogarth or a
Rowlandson.

Mrs. Trollope continued to record notes on the habits of the
American female and the rituals of her homelife, and as she explored
Cincinnati—and later Washington, Philadelphia and other cities—
she observed well. What she noted was all included in her famous
book, *Domestic Manners of the Americans,* which she wrote after the
fabulous, gaudy Bazaar failed to live up to her hopes.

The Trollopes had planned to make their fortune and then go back to England, leaving their son to run the place. All their available resources were sunk into the building of The Bazaar. And a bazaar it was, as described in a contemporary newspaper clipping: "Part Mosque, Egyptian in style, Moorish pilasters, arabesque windows, columns after the temple of Apollinoplis at Etfou . . . a curvilinear roof on which was featured the Turkish crescent." There was a circular staircase, a ballroom and an Exchange Coffee House. Hervieu did the interior decorating, and the whole "shebank," as the natives called it, was lighted by gas, the first such lighting in Cincinnati.

Mrs. Trollope, attacked by malaria, may soon have had doubts that the citizens of the town were ready for such grandeur, or whether they even knew the intrinsic value of anything.

Trouble came quickly to The Bazaar. The sheriff seized ten thousand dollars' worth of its goods—which were not selling anyway—on behalf of the building contractor, who claimed he had not been paid for his work. After this disaster Mrs. Trollope tried to present entertainments, such as *A Musical Fantasia*. This too failed, because the natives preferred obscene slapstick and ribald frontier humor.

Worse was to happen. As debts mounted, the sheriff seized all the household furnishings; and by March of 1830 there was nothing to do but to leave Cincinnati—and The Bazaar—behind. In time the place housed a church, then a hospital, and thirty years later a "Physico-Medical Institute" run by a quack doctor. It was claimed that no man or woman ever made a dollar in the building.

The courage of Mrs. Trollope during her strange odyssey is amazing. She, her artist and her children moved on to Washington, where she hoped to dig deeper into the American scene, as she was now determined to turn her notes into the record of a critical pilgrimage. Her eye remained keen, and what she wrote, with no hysterical distortion, about the lives and domestic lot of American women is well worth quoting.

Let me be permitted to describe the day of a Philadelphia lady of the first class. . . . She rises, and her first hour is spent in the scrupulously nice arrangement of her dress; she descends to her parlour neat, stiff, and silent; her breakfast is brought in by her free black footman; she eats her fried ham and her salt fish, and drinks her coffee in silence, while her husband reads one newspaper, and puts another under his elbow; and then, perhaps, she washes the cups and the saucers. Her carriage is ordered at eleven; till that hour she is employed in the pantry-room, her snow-white apron protecting her mouse-colored silk. Twenty minutes before her carriage should appear, she retires to her chamber, as she calls it, shakes and folds up her still snow-white apron, smoothes her rich dress, and with nice care, sets her elegant bonnet, and all the handsome et caetera, then walks down stairs, just at the moment that her free black coachman announces to her free black footman that the carriage waits. . . . It is to be imagined, that if fifty modifications of this charming young woman were to be met at a party, the men would dare to enter it reeking with whiskey, their lips blackened with tobacco, and convinced, to the very centre of their hearts and souls, that women were made for no other purpose than to fabricate sweetmeats and gingerbread, construct shirts, darn stockings, and become mothers of possible presidents. . . . Should the women of America ever discover what their power might be, and compare it with what it is, much improvement might be hoped for.

For some reason or other . . . a great number of young married persons board by the year, instead of "going to housekeeping," as they call having an establishment of their own. I can hardly imagine a contrivance more effectual for ensuring the insignificance of a woman, than marrying her at seventeen, and placing her in a boarding-house. Nor can I easily imagine a life of more uniform dullness for the lady herself; but this certainly is a matter of taste. I have heard many ladies declare that it is "just quite the perfection of comfort to have nothing to fix for oneself." Yet despite these assurances I always experienced a feeling which hovered between pity and contempt, when I contemplated their mode of existence. . . . She must rise exactly in time to reach the boarding table at the hour appointed for breakfast, or she will get a stiff bow from the lady president, cold coffee, and no egg. . . . The fasting, but tardy lady, looks around the table, and having ascertained that there was no egg left, says distinctly, "I will take an egg if you please. . . ." "There are no eggs, my dear." Whereupon the lady president evidently cannot hear, and the greedy culprit who has swallowed two eggs (for there are always as many eggs as noses) looks pretty considerably afraid of being found out. . . .

Mrs. Trollope sees the woman with her own house as little better off:

She puts on her scolloped black silk apron, walks into the kitchen to see that all is right, then into the parlour, where, having cast a careful glance over the table prepared for dinner, she sits down, work in hand, to await her spouse. He comes, shakes hands with her, spits, and dines. The conversation is not much, and ten minutes suffices for the dinner; fruit and toddy, the newspaper and the work-bag succeed. In the evening the gentleman . . . plays a snug rubber at a neighbor's. The lady receives at tea a young missionary . . . And so ends her day.

Frances Trollope left the United States in August of 1831, three years plus nine months after setting out for America with such high hopes. In England she found debts, creditors, ill children, and a doddering husband. Swiftly she wrote her book. With the publication of *Domestic Manners of the Americans,* she became famous. She earned enough money to live well for a time, but since she was voluble and extravagant, she embarked on a writing career. She wrote other travel books and many novels, illustrated by her traveling companion the French artist and by her son Tom, who also wrote.

Her book on America was her best. Was she fair? Was she accurate? From her position, yes, with just a touch of *haute noblesse.* Other works by English writers who visited America seem to bear out her viewpoint. Both a Captain Basil Hall, author of *Travels in North America* (1829), and later Charles Dickens, who was more of a cartoonist of the American scene than a true relater of facts, agreed with her impressions. Mrs. Trollope's account was superior to those of such visiting authors as Thomas Hamilton, Fanny Kemble, Harriet Martineau and Frederick Marryat.

The life-style that Mrs. Trollope first observed on the frontier along the Mississippi and the Ohio was nationwide. Frances Trollope was entertained by the best people in Washington, Philadelphia and New York; she visited theaters and danced at balls. The American way of life as it pertained to women did not impress her. She found an atrophied society set in its stubborn way, with no outlets for women's intellect and talents. It was a society dominated by hard-living, ill-mannered men with little interest in bettering the conditions of the female of any class. And women accepted this man's world in its totality.

Many editions of *Domestic Manners of the Americans* were printed. Today her book is as readable as ever; written by a desperate, debt-ridden woman of refinement and courage, it is a vital and honest book. No one embarking on the story of the Queen Bees can ignore it. It was the condition of women she pictured that the reformers who followed her—such as Lucy Stone and Susan B. Anthony—worked to correct.

How sharp she was regarding the sealed-in condition of American women:

> *They are quiet and orderly in their manners and habits, possess that sort of good housewifery that consists in being forever occupied about their household concerns. They are tender and attentive in the nursery, bustling and busy in the kitchen, unwearying at the needle and beautiful in the ballroom; but in the drawing-room—they are naught. . . . It is not that they do not dress; the women in proportion to their means dress more, or better—but generally speaking they want intelligence. What is far worse, they want grace. They want it in sitting, they want it in standing, they want it in expression, in accent, in tone. This is felt at every moment and scene, as it were, to neutralize every charm. Were they graceful, they would, from the age of fifteen to eighteen, be beautiful creatures indeed. They marry very early; once married, they seem to drop out of sight . . . out of all competition. . . .*

Americans responded harshly to Mrs. Trollope's book, as was to be expected. Editorials were written against it—she was denounced as a snobbish Briton, a busybody. But Mark Twain knew better:

Of all those tourists I like Dame Trollope best. She found a "civilization" here which you . . . could not have endured; and which you would not have regarded as a civilization at all. Mrs. Trollope spoke of this civilization of ours, in plain terms—plain and unsugared, but honest and without malice, and without hate. . . . She lived three years in this civilization of ours, in the body of it—not on the surface of it, as was the case with most of the foreign tourists of her day. She knew her subject well, and she set it forth fairly and squarely, without any weak ifs *and* ands *and* buts. *She deserved gratitude—but it is an error to suppose she got it.*

1.
The Revolt
of Lucy Stone

When told she had just given birth to a baby girl, the mother of Lucy Stone exclaimed, "Oh dear, I am sorry it's a girl. A woman's life is so hard."

Certainly it had been and still was hard for the mother who had borne eight children before Lucy. The night before Lucy was born in August 1818 on a farm a few miles from West Brookfield, Massachusetts, her mother had milked and stripped eight cows, besides doing her usual tasks.

Lucy Stone is best known today as the positively willful woman who insisted that married women keep their own last names instead of taking their husbands'. It's a cruel destiny that one of the first great organizers for women's rights should be remembered only for something that cannot compare to the great battles she fought and the converts she made for the cause of equal rights for women.

The Stones were of old native stock. When Gregory, the first to come over, arrived from England in 1635, already the desire to protect the rights of others was a family characteristic, for, sensitive to injustice, Gregory and his wife spoke in open court in defense of a woman accused of being a witch.

In 1664 Gregory Stone was one of a committee who presented a protest against New England's being ruled by a Royal Commission, because its inhabitants were then not represented in Parliament. Lucy's great-grandfather died at General Wolfe's taking of Quebec; her grandfather fought as a captain in Washington's army and later led four hundred men in a futile fight against entrenched bureaucrats in what has come down to us as Shays' Rebellion. The Stones seemed bred to an aggressive desire for freedom and justice.

Lucy's mother, Hannah Matthews Stone, had a higher-class family background than her husband, a tanner turned schoolteacher. She was related to such New England families as the Bowmans and the Forbushes. But Lucy remembered that "There was only one will in our house and that was my father's."

It was still a backwoods world, and Lucy and her siblings did the hard chores, such as chopping wood and herding cows. Before the age of machines, farm life meant the toil of hand labor. Women, like female farm animals, were seen as bearers of the young, and they had few legal rights. Domination by the man was not questioned—only endured.

When Lucy was growing up, she was shocked one day to read in the family Bible, "Thy desire shall be to thy husband, and he shall rule over thee." Later in life she claimed that this reading of holy duplicity changed her entire life. In her despair she even thought that she might do away with herself rather than be any man's slave. She said, "My mother always tried to submit. I never could." She must, she felt, question the Bible text, so she decided to go to college and study Hebrew and Greek. Her father thought her mad. Lucy had a temper, and she showed it. (She later decided to try to control her rages by never speaking when she flew into anger, and in time she became known for her gentle nature. She did realize her change, as the Psalms said, "Because I was flesh, and a breath that passeth away.")

As her mother grew weaker from overwork, Lucy took on the household chores while still attending a country school. At sixteen she was teaching school for a dollar a week and boarding around. She was short, stocky and pale—definitely not a country beauty. Her father, who seems to have been brutally frank, said Lucy had a "face like a blacksmith's apron; it keeps off the sparks [suitors]." She said her looks didn't matter, as she didn't intend to marry. Actually, before her marriage to Henry Blackwell in middle age, other men were in love with her, and she rejected other offers of marriage.

Lucy wanted to speak out to the larger world, to demand equal rights for women, after the fashion of two remarkable sisters, Sarah (1792–1873) and Angelina (1805–1879) Grimke, who came from a rich slave-owning South Carolina family. The sisters joined the American Antislavery Society and became public speakers against human slavery. They were perhaps the first women who dared to appear for a cause on all-male platforms. They were joined by another freedom fighter, Abby Kelley Forster, a Quaker from Worcester, Massachusetts, who gave her fortune for the antislavery cause. Together, this trio shattered the barriers that kept women from talking at public meetings.

Women who spoke out were attacked fiercely by the champions of society's despotism. A minister in Connecticut preached against Abby Kelley: "Thou sufferest that woman Jezebel, which calleth herself a prophetess, to teach, and to seduce my servants to commit fornication. . . . She comes with her brazen face, a servant of Satan in the garb of an angel of light, and tramples this commandment [St. Paul's] under her foot."

Lucy Stone, however, was impressed—exalted—by the actions of the Grimke sisters and Abby Kelley. She resented St. Paul—the first historic *macho*—and his bigoted rulings, "Let your women keep silence in the churches, for it is not permitted unto them to speak," and "I suffer not a woman to teach, not to usurp authority over man, but to be in silence."

Of the Grimke sisters she wrote to a brother, "I tell you they are first rate, and only help to confirm the resolution I have made to call no man master." In another letter she declared:

Only let females be educated in the same manner and with the same advantages that males have, and as everything in nature seeks its own level, I will risk that we would find out our own appropriate sphere. . . . Miss Adams [a fellow teacher] and I walked out to Springfield last Saturday, nearly twenty-five miles. We do not feel any inconvenience from it. . . . It was decided in our Literary Society . . . that ladies ought to mingle in politics, go to Congress, etc., etc.

Wurdemann Collection

Lucy Stone, in youth and old age; she used her maiden name only.

Lucy started classes at Mount Holyoke Seminary; three months later her mother's health broke, and Lucy went home to carry on. But she was determined to someday attend Oberlin College. The college had been founded in 1833 to train ministers and missionaries; in 1841 three women were the first females in the nation to receive a degree of Bachelor of Arts. Two years later Lucy Stone entered Oberlin. It had taken her nine years to save up funds to attend. She observed her family's reaction on her entering: ". . . long talked of and to Mother, long dreaded Oberlin . . . expense of getting here, including food $16.65. Rode day and night . . . was not sick coming over the lake."

Because Oberlin was a station on the "Underground Railway," the sight of fugitive slaves being smuggled to freedom was familiar to Lucy. She began a class to teach them to read and write. But the slaves in the school objected; it was not thought right for men— even slaves—to be taught by a woman. She convinced them, however, that this was a foolish idea.

In a letter home she wrote, "I have been weighed today. Weigh 119 pounds. . . . I have but very little headaches. . . . I have bought a fine big rocking chair . . . cost $4, but I shall get that amount of comfort out of it and rest my headaches."

As the first woman from Massachusetts to get a diploma, she felt she faced certain responsibilities. She was lecturing publicly on women's rights by 1847, the year of the first women's rights convention, held at Seneca Falls, New York. The rest of her life followed the same pattern: she lectured to and exhorted huge crowds; she was slandered and mocked everywhere—and she converted many to the cause. She continued to object to the conditions of women that Mrs. Trollope had observed:

In America, with the exception of dancing, which is almost wholly confined to the unmarried of both sexes, all the enjoyments of the men are found in the absence of the women. They dine, they play cards, they have musical meetings, they have suppers, all in large parties, but all without women. Were it not that such is the custom, it is impossible but

*that they would have ingenuity enough to find some expedient for
sparing the wives and daughters of the opulent the sordid offices of
household drudgery which they almost all perform in their families. Even
in the slave states, though they may not clear-starch and iron, mix
puddings and cakes one half of the day, and watch them baking the other
half, still the very highest occupy themselves in their household concerns,
in a manner that precludes the possibility of their becoming elegant and
enlightened companions. In Baltimore, Philadelphia, and New York, I
met with some exceptions to this, but speaking of the country generally, it
is unquestionably true.*

There are almost no references to prostitution in the literature
relating to Lucy Stone; the women around her remained Victorian
and Calvinist. Discussion of sexual morality was usually taboo on
public platforms. Yet the issue was vital. James McCabe, Jr., writing
in 1872, reports on "The Lost Sisterhood":

*In January, 1866, Bishop Simpson, of the Methodist Episcopal Church,
at a public meeting at the Cooper Institute, made the astounding
declaration that there were as many prostitutes in the city of New York as
there were members of the Methodist Church, the membership of which
at that time was estimated at between eleven and twelve thousand. In the
spring of 1871, the Rev. Dr. Bellows estimated the number of these
women at 20,000. The estimate of Dr. Bellows would brand one female
in every twenty-four, of all ages, as notoriously impure, and taking away
from the actual population those too old and too young to be included in
this class, the percentage would be very much larger—something like
one in every eighteen or twenty. The real facts are somewhat difficult to
ascertain. The police authorities boast that they have full information as
to the inmates of every house of ill-fame in the city, but their published
statistics are notoriously inaccurate. As near as can be ascertained, there
are about 600 houses of ill-fame in the city. The number of women living
in them, and those frequenting the bed-houses and lower class assignation houses, is about 5000. In this estimate is included about 700
waiter-girls in the concert saloons.*

This is the number of professional women of the town, but it does not include these who, while nominally virtuous, really live upon the wages of their shame, or the nominally respectable married and single women who occasionally visit assignation houses. It is impossible to estimate these, but it is believed that the number is proportionately small. Their sin is known only to themselves and their lovers, and they do not figure in the police records as abandoned women.

The fallen women include every grade of their class, from those who are living in luxury, to the poor wretches who are dying by inches in the slums. Every stage of the road to ruin is represented.

Lucy was, as far as American records show, the first married woman to keep her own name. *His* name was Henry Brown Blackwell, and he backed her in her crusade for equal rights for women, as seen in an agreement he signed on their wedding day: "I wish as a husband to renounce all privileges which the law confers on me which are not strictly mutual and I intend to do so." Abby's sister-in-law, Elizabeth Blackwell, was the first woman in the nation to get a medical degree and become a practicing physician. Another relative, Antoinette Brown Blackwell, was the first woman in the world to be ordained a Protestant minister.

Lucy Stone labored on, despite the view of many that hers was a quest doomed by its very absurdity to failure. She worked to change the picture for American women. She was a joiner: The New England Women's Club, New England Women's Press Association, Association of Collegiate Alumnae, The Grange, Christian Endeavor, and Women's Christian Temperance Union were all influenced by her. Two of the many she converted to the cause of women's rights were Susan B. Anthony and Julia Ward Howe ("The Battle Hymn of the Republic").

Late in life she wondered if she should have traveled abroad: "Oh why don't I do so many things . . . it is too late. But I have done what I wanted to do. I have helped the women." She also began signing her letters "Yours in good hope of the victory, not so far off as it was once."

Just a few days before she died, she wrote, "The [New York] *Herald* is an able paper. Will it use its great influence to help men and women go side by side to the ballot box?"

She died in the fall of 1893. Her last whispered words were "Make the world better."

2.
THE Mrs. Astor

So far as society and the sensational journalism of the day were concerned, there was only one Mrs. Astor: Mrs. William Astor of the 400. Both condemned and admired for her snobbish position and her indolence, she was the Queen Bee of what was considered the *crème de la crème* of society. She has been largely overlooked by social historians, in spite of the fact that she was the model for stylish clothes, and her elaborate rituals encouraged a general respect for grace and good manners and even led to standards of general cleanliness and sanitary plumbing. As did Lucy Stone, she saw her position with clarity and accuracy. She considered herself a pacesetter and lived in such a way that her influence changed the habits and the outlook of American women of all walks of life.

She was accused by yellow journalists of superficial sophistication because she spent a fortune on clothes, jewels, carriages and blooded horses, and in support of grand opera (then considered a snob's affectation). But her very notoriety helped spread her innovations to millions. Indoor plumbing was no longer considered effete, and the garment industry, created by German Jews and sweatshopped by Russian Jews fleeing the Tzars' pogroms, began to make available to shopgirls and housewives copies of better fashions. Of course the conditions under which these clothes were made in the sweatshops were appalling. Neither the women of Mrs. Astor's 400, who inspired the new ready-to-wear industry, nor those who bought the mass-produced clothes were really aware of the plight of the workers who made them. In his book *Lights and Shadows of New York Life* (1872), James D. McCabe, Jr., described the dreadful conditions under which the working woman suffered:

It is said that there are more than forty thousand women and girls in New York dependent upon their own exertions for their support. This estimate includes the sewing women, factory girls, shop girls, female clerks, teachers, and governesses. They all labor under two common disadvantages. They are paid less for the same amount of work than men, and being more helpless than men are more at the mercy of unscrupulous employers. The female clerks and shop girls receive small wages, it is true, but they are generally paid regularly and honestly. The sewing women and factory hands are usually the most unfortunate, and these constitute the great bulk of the working women. Many of these are married, or are widows with children dependent upon them for support.

The life of the New York working woman is very hard. She rises about daybreak, for she must have breakfast and be at her post by seven o'clock, if employed in a factory or work-shop. At noon she has a brief intermission for dinner, and then resumes her work, which lasts until six o'clock in the evening. You may see them in the morning, thinly clad, weary and anxious, going in crowds to their work. They have few holidays except on Sunday, and but few pleasures at any time. Life with them is a constant struggle, and one in which they are always at a disadvantage.

Even women who worked in better places sewing fashionable designs for upper-class women were not treated much better or paid much more. Only a romanticizing poet could have called them "the slaves of the needle."

Mrs. Astor, of course, had no intention of being a pacesetter for the middle classes; her turf was New York, Newport and Palm Beach. Yet she was one of the major influences in refining the uncouth habits of the nation. And while tiaras never became the fashion at country church suppers nor egret feathers among the fighters for women's rights, there was an evolution in female tailoring that could be traced to the poor and middle-class women's envy and admiration of the 400's elegant corseted forms, for the better styles in women's clothes were reproduced first from woodcuts, then from the rotogravures in the Sunday newspapers depicting the

The *Mrs. Astor. When she frowned, society trembled.*

wealthy—the Astors, the Vanderbilts, the Whitneys, the Goulds—
decked out in their finery from Worth's and other fashion designers.

Mrs. Astor was born Caroline Webster Schermerhorn in 1830. She
was no poor girl who married into wealth (society recombines every
generation, merging and changing). Her father was a speculator
whom *The Wealth and Biography of the Wealthy Citizens of New York* (1845)
listed as having a fortune of $500,000; today this would amount to
about $5 million.

Caroline's early photographs show her as strikingly handsome, if
no great beauty. In 1853 she married William Astor and so became
the great-granddaughter-in-law of the founding father of the Astor
fortune—John Jacob Astor, a fur trader who amassed his wealth by
skinning not only a good share of the wild animal life of the
continent, but also the Indians and the trappers. The Astors had
helped set the fashion for the furs: fox, wolf, mink, beaver (the latter
mostly for the high hats of the men).

Mrs. Astor studied her place in the pecking order of New York
society, noting that society's grotesque disparities and its dangers,
and started her slow, steady climb to the top. She gave fêtes and
dinners; she was seen in the Diamond Horseshoe of the Met; she
dined at Delmonico's; she received callers at her homes on Fifth
Avenue and in Newport—every action was socially calculated. By
the late 1880s she was honored by a column in the *New York Journal*
devoted to society doings, "Mrs. Astor's 400." Promoted by the
prancing little social pacesetter Ward McAllister, she was referred to
as "The Queen." "The Astor house has been, since 1870, the center of
fashionable life in America. How many thousands if not millions [sic]
have gazed upon it from outside with a feeling of curiosity and
interest."

In a way Mrs. Astor's 400 were always on display, exhibits of the
good life. The fact that the blue livery of the Astor servants matched
that of the staff in Windsor Castle could only enhance her fame. She
even had a throne—which delighted the mob—and those invited to
sit on the dais by her side considered themselves among the
anointed.

"Who should sit on the throne?" questioned one social commentator, Mrs. Drexel Lehr, who described it as "on a raised platform at one end of an enormous divan." The throne. No one ever thought of calling it anything else. It could accommodate only a limited number on those ample red silk cushions, and there were howls of acute disappointment from the rejected every year when seats were allotted.

Mrs. Astor also influenced interior decorating by using the Old Masters ("genuine oil paintings"), crystal candelabra, Tiffany lamps, and other elements of *art nouveau* decor. Her example encouraged young women of limited means to create their own Turkish corners with "Oriental rugs" (mostly from Belgium). The spittoon, that vulgar brass or silver article, was exiled to the den, attic or stable. Across the nation, wallpaper was copied from the Fifth Avenue patterns; Sears Roebuck offered "period dining room sets" vaguely Regency or Chippendale in style; from the Far West came "Spanish Mission" in fumed or golden oak. The hand-hewn plank tables and functional village-made chairs, sideboards and dressers were sent to the barn loft, only to become rare and valuable collectors' items several generations later. Silverware, furniture and articles of clothing were advertised and labeled as "The Fifth Avenue Set" or "The Society Set." The mysteries of the fish fork and the finger bowl were introduced to enhance gracious living. High button shoes with mother-of-pearl buttons were first seen in great numbers on both men and women in the Fifth Avenue Easter parades, at the Sheepshead racetrack, at Saratoga. They soon began to replace the local cobblers' boots (with no left or right foot pattern, they fitted *either* limb). The *Saturday Evening Post* ran stories about the success of a man who owned a dress suit which became a model for a bestseller, "Skinner's Dress Suit." It began to be called a *tux* because of the widespread belief that the high society of Tuxedo Park—a fashionable suburb of New York where elegant citizens rode horses instead of driving them—always dressed for dinner.

Certainly the revolution in food preparation that the Astor set introduced was long overdue; the national diet of campfire grease, singed meats, corn products, butchered hogs, and game brought to the table with buckshot still in it was sorely in need of change. What

was being replaced was aptly described by Frances Trollope in
Domestic Manners of the Americans:

> *In relating all I know of America, I surely must not omit so important a*
> *feature as the cooking. They consume an extraordinary quantity of*
> *bacon. Ham and beef-steaks appear morning, noon, and night. In*
> *eating, they mix things together with the strangest incongruity imagin-*
> *able. I have seen eggs and oysters eaten together; beef-steak with stewed*
> *peaches; and salt fish with onions. The bread, they rarely enjoy it*
> *themselves, as they insist upon eating horrible half-baked hot rolls both*
> *morning and evening. The butter is tolerable; but they have seldom such*
> *cream . . . the cows are very roughly kept, compared with ours. I never*
> *saw sea-cale, or cauliflowers, and either from the want of summer rain,*
> *or the want of care, the harvest of green vegetables is much sooner over*
> *than with us. They eat the Indian corn in a great variety of forms;*
> *sometimes it is dressed green, and eaten like peas; sometimes it is broken*
> *to pieces when dry, boiled plain, and brought to table like rice; this dish is*
> *called hominy. The flour of it is made into at least a dozen different sorts*
> *of cakes; but in my opinion all bad.*
>
> *I never saw turbot, salmon, or fresh cod. There is a great want of skill*
> *in the composition of sauces; not only with fish, but with every thing.*
> *They use very few made dishes. The game is very inferior to ours; they*
> *have no hares, and I never saw a pheasant.*
>
> *Every table has its dessert (invariably pronounced desart) which is*
> *placed on the table before the cloth is removed. They are "extravagantly*
> *fond," to use their own phrase, of puddings, pies, and all kinds of*
> *"sweets," particularly the ladies; but are by no means such connoisseurs*
> *in soups and ragouts as the gastronomes of Europe. Almost every one*
> *drinks water at table, and by a strange contradiction, in the country*
> *where hard drinking is more prevalent than in any other, there is less*
> *wine taken at dinner; in fact, the hard drinking, so universally*
> *acknowledged, does not take place at jovial dinners, but in solitary*
> *dram-drinking. Coffee is not served immediately after dinner, but makes*
> *part of the serious matter of tea-drinking, which comes some hours later.*
> *Mixed dinner parties of ladies and gentlemen are very rare, and unless*
> *several foreigners are present, but little conversation passes at table.*

It certainly does not, in my opinion, add to the well ordering of a dinner table, to set the gentlemen at one end of it, and the ladies at the other; but it is very rarely that you find it otherwise.

In *Lights and Shadows of New York Life* we get a glimpse of the new high society among "the best people," the society over which Mrs. Astor ruled:

New York has long been celebrated for its magnificent social entertainments. Its balls, dinner parties, receptions, private theatricals, picnics, croquet parties, and similar gatherings are unsurpassed in respect to show in any city in the world. Every year some new species of entertainment is devised by some leader in society, and repeated throughout the season by everyone who can raise the money to pay for it. . . .

Of late years it is becoming common not to give entertainments at one's residence, but to hire public rooms set apart for that purpose. There is a large house in the upper part of Fifth Avenue, which is fitted up exclusively for the use of persons giving balls, suppers or receptions. It is so large that several entertainments can be held at the same time on its different floors, without either annoying or inconveniencing the others.

The proprietor of the establishment provides everything down to the minutest detail, the wishes and tastes of the giver of the entertainment being scrupulously respected in everything. The host and hostess, in consequence, have no trouble, but have simply to be on hand at the proper time to receive their guests. This is a very expensive mode of entertaining, and costs from 5,000 to 15,000 dollars.

About nine o'clock magnificent equipages, with drivers and footmen in livery, commence to arrive, and from these gorgeous vehicles richly dressed ladies and gentlemen alight, and pass up the carpeted steps to the entrance door. . . . At the door stands someone to receive the cards of invitation. Once admitted, the ladies and gentlemen pass into the dressing rooms set apart for them. Here they put the last touches to their dress and hair and, the ladies having joined their escorts, enter the drawing room and pay their respects to the host and hostess.

Every arrangement is made for dancing. A fine orchestra is provided. There is very little dancing, however, of any kind, before midnight, the

*intervening time being taken up with the arrivals of guests and
promenading.*

*About midnight the supper room is thrown open, and there is a rush
for the tables, which are loaded with every delicacy that money can
buy. . . .*

*The richest and costliest of wines flow freely. At a certain entertain-
ment given not long since, 500 bottles of champagne worth over four
dollars each, were drunk. Some young men make a habit of abstaining
carefully during the day, in order to be the better prepared to drink at
night. The ladies drink almost as heavily as the men, and some of them
could easily drink their partners under the table.*

*After supper the dancing begins in earnest. If The German (a dance
step) is danced, it generally consumes the greater part of the evening. . . .
It is a dance in which the greatest freedom is permitted, and in which
liberties are taken and encouraged, which would be resented under other
circumstances.*

*The toilettes of the persons present are magnificent. The ladies are
very queens in their gorgeousness. They make their trains so long that
half the men are in mortal dread of breaking their necks over them; and
having gone to such expense in this quarter, they display the greatest
economy about the neck and bust. They may be in "full dress" as to the
lower part of their bodies, but they are fearfully undressed from the head
to the waist.*

Mrs. Astor herself was described as despotic, strong willed,
"motherly." For three decades she dominated sons, daughters and
grandchildren and continued to control what the *Journal* had to
admit was now "Mrs. Astor's 600." Records show that Mrs. Astor
and her group did support such efforts as reform in the sweatshops,
but they were against preaching in the streets to promote women's
sexual freedom and the unions' right to strike. She did charity work,
and there were stories of Mrs. Astor's helping a soiled tot blow his
nose and inspecting his injured unwashed knees. She is remembered
in memoirs as being "formidable and charming" at these tasks.
William Astor, her husband, kept a diary in which he recorded that
his wife was a "real woman in a real woman's atmosphere." While

J. P. Morgan, Henry Frick and the various early Rockefellers stuck closely to the past in their art collecting, women like Mrs. Havemeyer—a friend and contemporary of Mrs. Astor who bought paintings under the stern eyes of Mary Cassatt, companion of Degas—insisted on the introduction of the Impressionists into American drawing rooms and private collections. These pictures in many cases are now housed in great museums. (Gertrude Stein, in the same manner, encouraged the Cone sisters of Baltimore to acquire their huge collection of Matisses and Picassos.)

By the late 1890s Mrs. Astor was slipping from her social position. She was getting older, and society was becoming a looser organization which no longer adhered to her rigid ideas of "who was" and "who wasn't." New monied leaders from the West and the younger Vanderbilts and Goulds were producing a generation that did not need the approval of Mrs. Astor. An old order had to pass for a new order to appear. In the column "Chat From The Clubman," an 1880 *Town Topics* pointed out the signs of change:

> . . . *sympathize deeply with my friend . . . who says Society is going to the dogs—that is the Knickerbocker side of it, and "Good Gawd! dear boy, what other side is there?" Look at the list. How many of the swellest of the swell today were anything at all twenty years ago—fifteen years ago even? Where were the Vanderbilts, socially, even five years ago? The Astors had just fifteen years the social start. The Vanderbilts in fifteen more will have come up to an equality, and I prophesy they will eventually lead, partly because there is more gold on the young male, and more brass on the young female side of their house.*

There is the scent of sour grapes in this "chat," for Mrs. Astor still held considerable power.

One area in which she had a great deal of influence was in making divorce acceptable, first in her own circle and then across the nation. It began as a family matter. Her daughter Charlotte married J. Coleman Drayton of the Main Line, Philadelphia, and the couple had four children. After ten years of marriage, as one report had it, "Charlotte and Mr. Alsop Borrows by their indiscretions brought

down upon themselves the ungainly spectre of an outraged husband. . . ." There was a separation, and Charlotte paid her husband
$12,000 for the raising of their children. A year later, in 1892, the
husband, with two detectives as witnesses, followed his wife and
Borrows into the St. Pancras Hotel in London and gained evidence of
a physical affair. Certain letters were also published. Drayton even
challenged Borrows to a duel in France (the custom among gentlemen), but it never took place. Divorce proceedings dragged on for
years, with greedy lawyers reaping harvests, and it was all gleefully
reported in the press. It is hard to believe this gratuitous cruelty in
today's more permissive era of easy divorce proceedings.

When the divorce was at last granted in 1896, Charlotte forgot her
old lover and hurried off to marry a Scotsman, George Haig. She
brought him back with her to America, well aware that she was a
fallen woman, dishonored in the eyes of society.

Mrs. Astor faced this problem head on. Divorce was still looked
upon as a disgrace, and when adultery was the grounds, the divorced
woman was considered beyond the social pale. However, Mrs. Astor
stood by her erring daughter. As social commentator Julian Hawthorne (son of the author of *The Scarlet Letter*) put it in his autobiography, "Mrs. Astor made up her mind that her daughter should reign
at her side once more. . . . It does not excuse this lady to plead that
the culprit was her own daughter; nor that she believes in her
innocence. . . . For her, there should have been no daughter; no
innocence, nothing but a woman who had so far forgotten her social
duty as to let herself be accused and never have disproved the
accusation. Human nature, maternal sentiments have no place in the
case. She [Mrs. Astor] must remember only the obligations . . . and
condemn without mercy or reprieve."

If this sounds hardly human today, Hawthorne does express the
prevailing mood and attitude of some of "the best people," or at least
their public posture. In private, adultery and perverse pleasures
continued as usual.

Mrs. Astor, who was made of stern stuff, felt that her reign over
society was strong enough to overcome even the prejudices against a
divorced woman. She gave a huge social event in honor of her newly

divorced daughter and her new husband, George Haig; she drove her invitations like knife blades into the bodies of her friends. Attending, besides all of Mrs. Astor's court, was the Right Reverend Bishop Potter of the Diocese of New York. The eye of Mrs. Astor dared anyone to stare or offer any mild reminder of past sins.

Certainly this event and the consequent acceptance of Mrs. Haig back into the social stream did a great deal to encourage people to treat divorce less as a disgrace and more as a personal tragedy. Mrs. Astor's standing by her daughter Charlotte and upholding her right to be accepted among decent people struck the first telling blow against the ostracism of divorced women. The Women's Liberation movement today owes her some credit for giving the divorce bugaboo its first hard kick.

Mrs. Astor, it is clear, had a strong set of nerves. Her husband, William Astor, was a hedonist living cheerfully in the protective male shadow of the double standard. While a woman's reputation had to remain "pure as snow," untainted by public gossip, the man could be freely—even cheerfully—spoken of as a rounder, a skirt chaser, a turf hunter, and, at private clubs, a cocksman and a womanizer. During the last half of the nineteenth century and up to World War I, the male of social position was free to indulge in his sensuality and carnal desires without any social stigma.

Although she certainly knew that William Astor belonged to this free-living male set, Mrs. Astor ignored all talk about her husband's various affairs. Mrs. Lehr, a close friend (and a gossip), wrote in her memoirs, "When New York would ring with gossip concerning his [William's] latest doings and stories would circulate of wild parties on his yacht, his wife would never give vent to the faintest criticism of anything he did. She always spoke of him in terms of the greatest affection and admiration."

This she did until the year of her death, 1908.

3.
The Empress
of Feminism:
Susan B. Anthony

In her speech to the Syracuse Convention of 1852, Elizabeth Oakes Smith said:

> *Do we fully understand that we aim at nothing less than an entire subversion of the present order of society, a dissolution of the whole existing social compact?*
>
> *If any woman of genius is so untrue to herself as to say she should have been happier as an indoor, painstaking, fireside woman careful for the small savings of a household . . . she is from some cause disqualified for the holding of God's beautiful and abundant gifts. . . .*

And in 1860 Elizabeth Cady Stanton declared:

> *Prejudice against color, of which we hear so much, is no stronger than that against sex. It is produced by the same cause, and manifested very much in the same way. The Negro's skin and the woman's sex are both* prima facie *evidence that they were intended to be in subjection to the white Saxon man.*

These women were radicals, and the figurehead of their cause was Susan Brownell Anthony.

Every movement has a figurehead, and many times he or she outshines many others who may be equally important and as valuable to the cause. In Susan's case, however, her position as the keystone in the fight for women's rights was well deserved. Known by some as "The Champion of a Lost Cause," she fought hard in her battles for the emancipation of the American woman; she never gave up warring against unfair laws, venal government and the ingrained bigotry of her times.

Susan was born in 1820 into a Quaker family in Adams, Massachusetts. She grew up in the tight homily-edged rituals of that creed, using the *thee* and *thou* form of speech. She dressed in somber Quaker garments which served, in their monotony, to guard one against pride. There was not much laughter or frivolity—only a great deal of hard farmwork. Quaker women were as exploited by their men as any other class of women in the nation; however, female education, at least among the Anthonys, was not neglected. Susan was bright, and by the age of five she had learned to read and write. There was a strange streak in her—a search for the infinite diversity of life. She wanted to study subjects that girls were supposed to ignore, such as "advanced" arithmetic. At Miss Deborah Moulson's Select Seminary for Females, Susan was soon in rebellion. However, in the panic of 1838, her father went bankrupt, so she could no longer

Library of Congress

A women's rights group, photographed by Matthew Brady. Susan B. Anthony is seated second from right.

attend the school. The family moved to the sadly named town of
Hardscrabble, New York, to try farming again. To help out finan-
cially, Susan began to teach school, almost the only work open for a
bright country girl who didn't want to work as a governess or a
housemaid. She replaced a male teacher whose salary had been ten
dollars a week, but Susan was paid five dollars a week.

Working did not cause her to conform to society, for she never
feared speaking out against injustice and low pay for women. There
was little of the Quaker left in her by then. She was tall and not a
beauty, and it was said she "thought like a man." Later, in a better
teaching job, she was called "the smartest woman in the Canajoharie
Academy."

Susan was a joiner. Abolitionists became her friends, and she
worked against black slavery. She joined the Daughters of Temperance because she was aware, as Mrs. Trollope had been, of the
nation's addiction to strong drink, including high-proof corn
pressings, bourbon, hard cider, rum and brandy.

After 1855 the rights of women became Susan's special crusade.
She joined forces with and lived with Elizabeth Cady Stanton, one of
the cosponsors of the Seneca Falls Convention for Women's Rights.
They wore bloomers—those most daring pants—to advocate dress
reform for all their sex, and they cut their hair short. (They later gave
up dress reform because it was treated as freakish and could have
harmed the cause; controversy over dress was too easy to caricature.)

The cause that Susan led focused on forcing the New York State
Legislature to change the legal status of women. A married woman's
right to keep her own earnings, to regulate her personal property, to
have joint guardianship over her children, and to demand an economic standard equal to a man's—these were the aims of the
convention. It was a long fight to get the rights of women made into
law, but by 1860 the legal changes had begun in Albany.

Meanwhile, nasty attacks were made on Susan and her groups.
The New York World, a popular gutter press, launched loud, unseemly
attacks on Miss Anthony's personal appearance: "Susan is lean,
cadaverous and intellectual with the proportions of a file, and the

voice of a hurdy-gurdy . . . " The most dastardly assault was calling her "intellectual." Women were mothers, wives or house slaves, vessels for a man's sexual demands, creatures of prayer. "To milk a cow, hoe a straight patch of beans—that's enough for a woman," wrote one Indiana farmer. And in the South there was a popular slogan for keeping a woman contented and busy: "Keep 'em barefoot and keep 'em pregnant." Ministers joined in the attacks on Susan and her reformer groups, declaring that they went against God's plan: "Woman Suffrage: The Reform Against Nature" stated one minister's publication. But an unknown woman reformer summed up many a woman's view in a fragment of a letter: "Men have the idea that their brains and their right to appear the lords of creation resides in-their balls."

The Civil War caused a setback in the progress Susan had made in the area of legal rights for women. The New York State Legislature repealed some of the rights it had given women over their children in the 1850s. But Susan had other concerns. Lincoln had not gone to war to free the slaves: he had been fighting to preserve the Union. Now, in running for reelection, he needed something free of controversy to attract attention, so he produced the Emancipation Proclamation freeing the slaves. Susan saw her opportunity; she cried out in public: "Free the women as well as the slaves if this is a government of the people, by the people!" Susan B. Anthony insisted that women were people. Susan and the leaders of the women's rights movement saw that they had to demand a constitutional amendment that would actually abolish slavery and give full rights to white and black women as well as black men. Who could deny them these rights now?

There were marches, speeches, organizations, many printed documents, many debates. The Thirteenth Amendment, giving full rights to all, passed with the women's help. But when Susan and other women read the contents of the proposed Fourteenth Amendment, they went into shock. All civil rights were reserved only for previously disenfranchised male citizens! Susan began to cry out in protest. She called for a one-word change: strike out the word male—pass the amendment without that hurtful term and blacks and women would have the vote. It was that simple.

One of those against changing the amendment to favor women was Horace Greeley, the celebrated newspaper personality. He has remained a folk hero for his remark "Go west, young man," but he was also an eccentric and sometimes a fool as well. He was soon to lose his mind and sink into debased senility, but at the time of the battle over omitting the word *male* from the Fourteenth, he was still mettlesome enough to take Susan B. Anthony to task.

"Miss Anthony, you are aware that the ballot and the bullet go together. If you vote, are you prepared to fight?"

Susan answered calmly, "Certainly, Mr. Greeley. Just as you fought in the last war—at the point of a goose-quill pen."

Greeley and his kind blocked the vote for women in New York State, and in the end the Fourteenth Amendment became law as written, affecting only the "previously disenfranchised male citizens."

In 1872 Susan was still battering away at the injustice of the Fourteenth, and also the Fifteenth, which guaranteed the right to vote to all men regardless of race. She boldly, publicly cast a vote in the presidential election—and was promptly arrested for violating the Constitution. Her fine for this unladylike deed was one hundred dollars and costs; she refused to pay.

She edited a newspaper called *Revolution* which failed. Susan labored to pay its debts; although she was poor, she eventually managed to raise nearly ten thousand dollars.

For Susan, it was self-realization that mattered. In the paper she printed a slogan that became her philosophy: "Men their rights, and nothing more: Women their rights, and nothing less."

She continually demanded sexual equality, the vote for women, and the abolition of legal differences between the rights of men and the rights of women.

In 1904 Susan, then eighty-six, saw the formation of the International Women's Suffrage Alliance. Two years later, attending her last convention, she told the cheering women, "The fight must not stop.

You must see it does not stop!" At a last dinner in her honor in Washington, she boldly stated, "Failure is impossible!"

She was right. Thirteen years after her death, on May 21, 1919, the "Susan B. Anthony Amendment," giving women their full rights as citizens, became part of the United States Constitution.

4.
In Search
of New Worlds

"What makes the reading of Henry James's novels seem so far from our own world," F. Scott Fitzgerald stated, "is that James wrote of a women's world that had disappeared. It was narrow and socially ingrown, even precious in the wrong sense. It was a world of overly literate American ladies who felt that America was materialistic and crude."

They went to live in Florence and Rome, these women named Cassat, Sargent, Wharton, Smith. Like the Morgans, they took the grand tours. Hawthorne knew them in Rome as female expatriates. They were artists, writers of travel books, students of papal Italy. Edith Wharton analyzed these women mercilessly in her various studies of the American colony in France.

But, as Fitzgerald pointed out, the Great War brought an end to their importance. Their children and grandchildren belonged to the age of Herbert Hoover, of nightclub jazz, of the tennis courts at Santa Barbara.

In some cases, the older exiles were rich American girls marrying good or bad European titles. Such title-hunting evoked much flag-waving journalism in American newspapers and many sardonic drawings by Charles Dana Gibson and other graphic artists, drawings of American heiresses seeking the coat-of-arms of a duke, a lord or a count. This bartering for prestige did help Americans enter a larger world, but it also undermined the position of the Astors and the Vanderbilts.

The story of the Leiter family of Chicago is a fine example of the way determined American women widened their social world. Levi

Leiter, with his Jewish background, saw his daughter Mary wed to Lord George Nathaniel Cuzon, Fourth Baron of Scarsdale. At his side she became Vicereine of India amidst a Kiplingesque welter of elephants, saffron dust, diamonds and British scarlet drawn up in rigid ranks with honored battle flags.

Levi Zeigler Leiter (the original family name was Leitersburg) was born in Maryland in 1834. He began his career as a clerk in a country general store filled with mule harnesses, dry goods, notions, coal-oil cans, wheels of jack cheese, and various foods that were sold from open bins. In 1885 Levi moved to Chicago, then known as Mudville, where he rose from a clerk's position to a partnership in Cooley, Wadsworth & Company. Another partner was Marshall Field. Ten years later Leiter and Field bought control of the dry goods firm (the merchandise now included cotton, silk and wool) of Potter Palmer, whose wife was to become one of the Queen Bees of Chicago. They operated as Field & Leiter until Levi left for the more rewarding world of speculation in land values and business properties and of the manipulation of corporate stocks.

In 1866 Levi married Mary Theresa Carver, a schoolteacher. Their three daughters became heroines to the vast number of newspaper readers avidly interested in American girls who made it across "the big pond" to success in Europe: Mary became Lady Cuzon, Nancy married a Major Campbell who was in line for Duke of Argyll's title, and Marguerite became Lady Suffolk.

Surprisingly for a schoolteacher, Mary Theresa was a social fumbler who became known for such malapropisms as "My husband went to a fancy dress ball in the garbage of a monk" and "There were statues in the nickies [wall openings]."

But one couldn't laugh at the Levis' fortune of $30 million. The family, with the three girls in tow, moved to an ornate mansion on Dupont Circle in Washington, D.C. There they could look over good marriage prospects for the girls.

It was Baron Speck von Sternberg, First Secretary to the Imperial German Embassy, who introduced the thirty-one-year-old Cuzon to Mary Leiter. Cuzon was a man to watch, for his political promise was bright. A bit of a snob, pompous yet charming, he needed a rich wife,

Wurdemann Collection

Mary Leiter, an American heiress who married into British aristocracy.

as was the tradition in the British diplomatic service. The *New York World*, which under the first Pulitzer was a newspaper devoted to explaining the reasons why important young Englishmen of good families so often married American girls, hoped "in this case it was for Mary's beauty and not her money."

The wedding—the families ignored such journalistic gaucherie—was a great event. English relatives, titled and otherwise, were brought over by Mr. Cuzon. The wife of President Cleveland attended (in a little yellow bonnet), as well as Mrs. Yang, wife of the Chinese ambassador (she wore apple blossoms on her head).

A reporter noted that the bridegroom "was a very pleasing prospect." The *New York Journal,* however, reported that Mrs. Cuzon brought to the bridegroom a private fortune in American securities amounting to millions.

The Leiter girls are important to the American scene because they broke the hold of the long-entrenched social queens and opened the way for minority women (wealthy ones, at least) to live in a world long barred to them. They also helped to bring England and America closer together, partially healing the bitter memory of revolution.

Nancy Langhorne, better known as Lady Astor, was another American exile, but of a far different sort. She was born in 1879 to Chiswell Dabney Langhorne and his wife, born Nancy Keene, whom he married when she was sixteen. Chiswell Langhorne was at various times a hotel janitor, a slave-owning tobacco grower, a gambler and, finally, a contractor on the railroad, a position in which he made

Lady Astor,
born Nancy Langhorne.

Library of Congress

money. In all, the parents produced eleven children. Daughter Nancy was the first woman to achieve prominence as an able elected woman politician, and one of her sisters, Mrs. Charles Dana Gibson, was the first model for the Gibson Girl.

At age twenty Nancy married Robert Gould Shaw, but he, having no sense of obligation, drank and chased women. Nancy, already a hard advocate of women's rights, divorced him in 1903.

Nancy moved to England, where she lived as a bachelor girl, in her own establishment. On one sea trip she met Viscount Waldorf Astor, reportedly one of the richest men in the world at the time, and married him; in 1907 she became a British citizen. When Astor's father died, he entered the House of Lords. By that time Nancy had produced five children. Restless and active, she ran for Parliament in 1919, and she won.

She had a rasping tongue and a despotic wit, which the lower classes seemed to enjoy. She was ill-mannered and daring. As she told King Edward VII, the playboy and hedonist, when he asked her to play cards, "I don't know the difference between a king and a knave." One either admired Lady Astor or disliked her tart and rather snobbish ways.

Her importance to social change was that although she was not the first woman to take politics seriously, she was one of the best known, and so encouraged others to follow her down the corridors of power to elected office. Nancy held her seat in Parliament until 1945, but by then her sense of public attention and outspokenness had damaged her reputation.

She was well aware of her own faults: "My vigor, vitality and cheek repel me. . . . I am the kind of woman I would run from." And many did, including Churchill and Shaw.

Nancy lived into her eighties, and, whatever her faults, she was the new kind of woman, a twentieth-century figure who dared speak out with a boldness that no one in her social position in America would have found proper before 1900. She wanted to outlaw war, and she favored easy divorces and full rights for women, including the vote.

5.
Doctor in Skirts

While most people are familiar with Clara Barton, who founded the American Red Cross after experiencing the bloody years of the Civil War, few are even aware of Dr. Mary Edwards Walker (1832–1919), the first woman physician to serve the U.S. Army. President Lincoln nominated her for the highest military award of the nation: the Medal of Honor. After Lincoln's assassination, President Andrew Johnson, in November of 1865, presented the medal.

But then in 1916 an Army review board reported that "Dr. Walker was not legally a member of the Army" and withdrew the award. Perhaps, some said, there was more to it than a technicality; Dr. Walker had been a women's rights advocate who kept her maiden name after marriage. And in a day when divorce was frowned upon, she had divorced her husband on the grounds of adultery; she had also appeared in public in men's attire and had spoken out strongly against capital punishment, child labor, drugs, alcohol and tobacco.

For the first three years of the Civil War, Dr. Walker served as an unpaid nurse (as did Walt Whitman), all the time seeking an appointment as an Army surgeon. She did receive a contract, but not a commission; no woman officially served in the armed forces of that war. Dr. Walker rode military ambulances and worked on Army hospital trains and ships. She also seems to have been the first woman to ride in a military observation balloon, spying on enemy-held territory.

She was on the field at Gettysburg through those fearful days when the casualties on each side numbered more than seventy thousand men. In the nights the cries of the wounded filled the hot July darkness; the morning revealed the dead and dying. Hospital conditions were dreadful; amputations were done by lantern light on farm tables. Still, Dr. Mary Edwards Walker worked on, tending wounded men from both sides.

In 1864 she performed operations on battle wounds for an Ohio regiment. Always in danger (and not just from the infection of blood poisoning), she was eventually captured by rebel forces and held prisoner for four months.

Years later, when the medal for her services was revoked, she refused to give it up, wearing it proudly and defiantly. But a relative did insist that her heart broke "at the treatment she got."

What actually killed her (her kind do not let their hearts break) was a trip she made to Washington in 1917 to try to persuade the members of Congress to restore her right to the Medal of Honor. They avoided any real action. The Army Board of Correction of Military Records solemnly reported that "Dr. Walker had been discriminated against because she was a woman, but that the true fact was the Army did not legally accept women to serve in the military." (However, in 1917 there were women serving in the American Army.)

While visiting the Capitol, Dr. Walker fell on the high bank of steps and broke her hip. She never fully recovered from this injury and died in near poverty in 1919 at her home in Oswego, New York.

Dr. Mary Edwards Walker's story might have ended here, in the shabby treatment of a heroic woman by her own government. But sixty years later a Ms. Anne Walker, a great-grandniece of Dr. Walker, took up the fight to have the Medal of Honor legally awarded to the battlefield surgeon who had treated wounded at Bull Run and Gettysburg. Anne Walker fought the tangle of Pentagon desk generals and congressional committees for four years. Lesiglators and military officials burrowed deep into their offices to avoid her and her cause.

In 1977 the Army Board admitted that Dr. Walker had been the victim of sex discrimination, and Secretary of the Army Clifford Alexander, Jr., fully approved the Board's action and cited Dr. Walker "for gallantry and bravery." The Senate and the House woke up, and after Edward M. Brooke introduced the resolution in the Senate, they recommended the restoration of the Medal of Honor.

Great-grandniece Anne Walker expressed her victory as "a case of a white President of the South and a black male senator from the North being concerned with a Civil War story about a woman."

Today, if you can gain entrance to the closed Armed Forces Medical Museum in Washington (where the bones of General Sickles's amputated leg are honored in a splendid little coffin), you can see nearly all the surviving material evidence of Dr. Walker. Her medical kit is there, and her Union officer's uniform, trousers and all. Her Medal of Honor is displayed in the Oswego Historical Museum, along with a photograph of her wearing it.

6.
Margaret Fuller's "Higher Sentiments"

For anyone interested in a wildly romantic personality combined with an intelligent, probing mind, Margaret Fuller is a perfect subject. An experienced traveler, she was far different from Susan B. Anthony, who always regretted that she had not gone abroad to see some of the rest of the world. "Why," Margaret wrote, "should American women be satisfied with the common routines of living?"

Margaret Fuller was born in 1810 into a proper New England family; her father was a congressman. She was not a great beauty like the women in the Flaxman engravings she admired, but she was brilliant and would later be identified as a bluestocking. She had a resourceful mind and expressed herself well. She was once introduced to Emerson as "a most brilliant talker." As a very young woman she debated the ideas of Emerson, Thoreau and Alcott (father of Louisa May) in Cambridge, Massachusetts, where her father, Timothy Fuller, had returned to write a history of America. He taught Margaret Latin when she was still a lisping baby, and in her childish prayers she would state, "O God if thou are Jupiter."

She was an impetuous, impassioned girl. At school she dominated all the other girls, falling into swoons to get her way and banging her head against the fireplace when angry. The girls called her "The Bandit's Bride" when she wove flowers into her hair. Her days were carefully planned. She rose at dawn, walked an hour, then practiced the piano. Next she read philosophy (Goethe was a favorite author); she also studied French, Greek and Italian. Later, after she had played the piano again and sung, she finished the day by writing in her journal. To earn a living after her father died, Margaret taught girls,

introducing them to the works of Schiller and Goethe, and of
Petrarch and Tasso in Italian.

Margaret differed from the social patterns noticeably enough to
frighten off the average man. She had deep yearnings, wild romantic
fantasies in which she imagined herself in some Icelandic saga or
some novel of George Sand. She also saw herself as the goddess Isis.
She wrote in her journal: "Iphigenia, I was not born in vain. If only
for the tears I have shed with thee!"

Margaret Fuller, a formidable intellectual of her time.

She believed in omens and signs. To doubters, Margaret explained that she was a pearl; she said that "in the slime of the oyster's body the true jewel is found." Yet she felt that her mysterious fire had little chance to flare in a man's world. How could an imaginative female survive? She said, "American men? No variety of depth and tone."

She felt that the words of her idol, George Sand, summed up her feelings:

That women differ from men, that heart and intellect are subject to the laws of sex . . . I do not doubt . . . But ought this difference, so essential to the general harmony of things, constitute a moral inferiority? . . .

For a woman to cease being a woman is productive only of inferiority. . . .

Education will in time be the same for men and women, but it will be in the female heart par excellence, as it always has been, that love and devotion, patience and pity, will find their true home. On woman falls the duty, in a world of brute passions, of preserving the virtues of charity and the Christian spirit. . . . When women cease to play that role, life will be the loser.

I maintain that the old and ugly who buy young bodies for cash are not indulging in "love," and that what they do has nothing in common with the Cyprian Venus, with groined arches or infinities or male or female! It is something wholly against nature, since it is not desire that pushes the young girl into the arms of the ugly dotard, and an act in which there is neither liberty nor the sanctity of nature. . . .

One of the men impressed by her abilities was Horace Greeley. Although he was not much of an advocate of women's rights, Greeley saw the merit in Margaret and aided her in her endeavors by giving her books to review and setting her to writing on literary subjects.

By 1844 Margaret was in New York, living in the editor's home and working on the staff of the *Tribune*. She visited prisons and slums. She traveled to Chicago and then on into Wisconsin to view the settlers. As a critic she knocked over old idols; she said that Longfellow had "a hollow second-hand sound" and that "Emerson did not lie along the ground long enough."

By 1846 she had realized that America wasn't yet ready for the higher sentiments. Like Alexander the Great she was looking for new worlds, if not to conquer, then to impress herself upon.

In those days, to travel alone across the seas was something no woman did. Even a generation later, Henry James could still record in his notebook:

> Hotel Richemont, Lausanne, August 4th. . . . last evening at Ouchy, Miss R said . . . "A girl should be shown Europe——or taken to travel——by her husband. She has no business to see the world before he takes her . . . he initiates her" . . . a possible idea for a little tale. The girl's life—— waiting——growing older——death. The husband comes in the form of death, etc.

But for Margaret Fuller it was not death, but life opening up. She could speak the languages she had studied so hard, but she was still the observer: "Why bind oneself to a central, or any, doctrine? How much nobler stands a man entirely unpledged, unbound?"

When she invaded Europe, she wrote letters back to the *Tribune* which were to become the book *At Home and Abroad*. Thomas Carlyle wrote that her "courage was high and clear . . . a truly heroic mind altogether unique, as far as I know, among the writing women of this generation."

In Europe she moved among her equals. Chopin ran through a piano work for her; she held the hand of George Sand. Concerning her countrymen, however, she commented that the American tourists were "booby truants." Clearly she was a snob, and a very outspoken one. She remained erudite and emancipated, but she did join Mazzini's fight to free and unite Italy in his "God and the People party." To Margaret they were like the Abolitionists back home.

In her passionate inner self she felt that she had not been attractive to American men, even those of the inner Emerson circle. But in Italy romance came to her as if out of one of the popular romances of the period. The Marchese Ossoli fell in love with this clever, intelligent American. He was a nobleman, ten years older than she, a fighter for Italian unification, a man overflowing with the Latin charm that Americans expect. Her love was a sensibility welling up from within her—a passion, a mesmeric compulsion that achieved its goal when she became his mistress.

Their sexual union produced a child, and they were married, even though Margaret did not approve of the ritual, finding it more of a bind than a tie.

In 1850 the short-lived Roman Republic was overthrown by reactionaries. Margaret, with her husband and baby, decided to sail to America. As in the romantic tales written by Poe and Mary Shelley, the ship ran into a storm off Fire Island, and the three of them drowned in the resulting shipwreck.

It is the tragic climax to Margaret Fuller's complex life that has kept her memory alive. Her literary criticism remains unread, although it can be compared favorably with Poe's. As an outspoken advocate of women's rights, she was less active than others in the field, but she did make vital contributions in the battle to free women from the snares and nets of a man-dominated world. In a Conversation on Education she once expressed the view that what we can do for ourselves and others is to consider impulse and spontaneity the proper agents for action.

For all her indignant petulance and frenetic activity, she was an outstanding and talented woman.

Margaret affected people by her vigor, her drive and her keen intelligence. Hers was the image of a woman living life as freely as she wanted, striking out against the superficial boundaries of her time. She was the type of woman who wanted to be treated as an equal. She was resented by many men who felt that she tried to stretch her abilities as an intellectual woman too far; that is, they thought she espoused male values. James Russell Lowell considered her spiteful and egotistic; Poe praised her as a critic but damned her as a careless stylist in her writing; Emerson was a hot-and-cold admirer: "Strange, cold-warm, attractive-repelling conversation with Margaret . . . whom I sometimes love; yet whom I freeze and who freezes me to silence when we promise to come nearest." The character

Zenobia in Hawthorne's *The Blithedale Romance* was modeled after her.

Margaret Fuller's relationship with the world is best summed up by her comment, repeated to Thomas Carlyle, "I accept the universe."

To which Carlyle replied: "By God! She'd better!"

7.
More Wrongs than Rights

Early in the nineteenth century, wives came up against the egocentric-male–oriented American legal system, a carryover from English common law. The law said that a husband had the legal right to beat his wife "with a reasonable instrument." In one wife-beating case, a judge, asked to define a "reasonable instrument," explained: "Gentlemen of the jury . . . a stick no thicker than my thumb comes clearly within that description." In painful perplexity, a group of women protestors asked to have his thumb measured.

There were other legal opinions, only slightly more favorable to the woman. The male's case was always bolstered by a commentary added to the text of the general court by Judge Sewell of Massachusetts, a Puritan who had helped condemn witches: "Every married woman shall be free from bodily correction or stripes by her husband *unless* it is in his own defense." A husband could thus claim assault, safeguarded by the word *unless*.

In 1848 a woman advocate of women's rights in New York State reported that "a husband's supremacy was often enforced in the rural districts by corporal chastisement," and this was considered by most people as "quite right and proper."

Alexis de Tocqueville, a careful observer of early nineteenth-century America, saw the American woman's problems from a different angle:

> . . . before an American girl arrives at the marriageable age, her
> emancipation from maternal control begins: she has scarcely ceased to be
> a child when she already thinks for herself, and acts on her own impulses.
> . . . An American girl scarcely ever displays that virginal softness in the

*midst of young desires or that innocent and ingenuous grace which
usually attends the European woman in the transition from girlhood to
youth. Like the young women of Europe she seeks to please, but she
knows precisely the cost of pleasing. If she does not abandon herself to
evil, at least she knows that it exists; and she is remarkable rather for
purity of manners than for chastity of mind.*

But de Tocqueville was also aware of certain problems:

*. . . If an unmarried woman is less constrained there than elsewhere, a
wife is subjected to stricter obligations. The former makes her father's
house an abode of freedom and of pleasure; the latter lives in the home of
her husband as if it were a cloister . . . perhaps not so contrary as may be
supposed . . . that the American woman should pass through the one to
arrive at the other. . . .*

    *The Americans are a puritanical people and a commercial nation;
their religious opinions as well as their trading habits consequently lead
them to require much abnegation on the part of woman and a constant
sacrifice of her pleasures to her duties. . . . Thus in the United States the
inexorable opinion of the public carefully circumscribes woman within
the narrow circle of domestic interests and duties and forbids her to step
beyond it.*

In the nineteenth century wives had almost no legal rights. A wife
was forbidden to make contracts; she could not sue in court, but she
could be sued. She could not make a legally valid will without her
husband's permission—unless she made him her sole heir. A married
woman's personal property, along with her private income and
earnings, belonged to her husband. Control of the children was his
alone while he lived; and when he died he could, by the terms of his
will, give them away to relatives or strangers. If the wife died, the
husband had the use of her property during his lifetime, whether or
not there were children. But when the male died, the widow had the
right to live in the house rent-free for only forty days.

Nineteenth-century prints and engravings show women attending
lectures and sermons. But the women did not speak, because public

In the mid-nineteenth century, women could attend meetings but were not allowed to appear as speakers.

talks by women were considered indecent. Since they couldn't speak in public, some of them, like Louisa May Alcott, took up writing. Harriet Beecher Stowe wrote what was to be the most popular novel of the first half of that century, and Julia Ward Howe produced the text to the most stirring hymn of its time, "The Battle Hymn of the Republic." Yet as gentle a person as Charles Lamb found the emergence of women scribblers revolting: "The woman who lets herself be known as an author invites disrespect. . . . "

Prints and engravings also show how American women were imprisoned by their clothes. Mrs. Amelia Bloomer, the editor of the first woman's newspaper, *The Lily,* advocated (but did not invent) a garment that was named after her. A short skirt over a baggy pantslike garment that reached the ankles, it was worn in the streets in full view of the public. The original bloomer was actually invented

Amelia Bloomer did not invent this famous costume. She did, however, advocate it for public wear, and it was named after her.

in 1841 in western New York by Mrs. Elizabeth Smith Miller, the daughter of an Abolitionist. A self-assured outdoor woman given to taking long walks, she designed a garment that made walking easier in those days of bustles and floor-reaching, dust-gathering skirts. It in no way resembled the bloomers worn by high school girls in gym classes of the 1930s. Mrs. Miller's bloomers consisted of a shirt-type jacket, a mid-calf–length skirt with no petticoats, and the actual trousers (one blushed to say the word in mixed company), which came down to the shoe tops, thus covering any possibly alluring section of the female limb.

Lucy Stone sewed her first bloomers for home use but soon began to wear them outdoors. Her husband, Henry B. Blackwell, admitted that they were improper: "When I first saw it, I acknowledge my taste recoiled from the novelty. I felt a shock . . . as a figure which seemed neither man nor woman approached me."

The bloomer women were mocked wherever they went, and crowds followed them and jeered. Most wearers soon gave up the freedom dress out of frustration at the petty persecution.

Even Lucy Stone was wearing a long dress by 1854. One of her followers had written: "For your own sake, lay aside the shorts . . . not for the sake of the cause, nor for any sake but your own, take it off. . . . What is physical freedom compared with mental bondage? By all means have the new dress made longer." Lucy later wrote that Mrs. Miller herself wore the bloomers for a much longer time than any of the other women, "But, little by little, her skirts lengthened. . . ."

Yet a first blow had been struck against the cloth armor with its rows of buttons and its whalebone corsets.

8.
The Other Victoria

. . . The great political or social agitator is most often a bird of curious plumage, all of whose feathers, even the queerest, play their part in flight. . . .

Henry James

She was the first woman even nominated by a political party for the presidency of the United States; she campaigned vigorously for the office. More realistically speaking, she was an ardent suffragist who published pamphlets, as well as a popular radical magazine. She started a successful brokerage office on Wall Street and advanced women's rights by exposing the adulterous adventures of the most eminent American clergyman of her day—Henry Ward Beecher, a man Abraham Lincoln once called "the greatest preacher since St. Paul."

Victoria Claflin Woodhull certainly belongs among the Queen Bees, for she was one of the strongest proponents of the burgeoning Women's Liberation movement. Yet she was an adventuress, a confidence woman, and perhaps even a prostitute at one point in her varied and wild career. She practiced what she preached: sexual freedom outside of marriage (labeled "free love"). "All talk of women's rights is moonshine," Victoria insisted; "women have *every* right. They have only to exercise them. That's what we're [she and her sister Tennessee] doing."

Whereas the earlier women's rights speakers had soft-pedaled the sexual question, she was outrageously frank. In 1872, while addressing three thousand people in Steinway Hall in New York, Victoria loudly proclaimed, "I have an inalienable right, constitutional and

Ross Collection

Victoria Woodhull, the first woman to run for the American presidency.

natural right, to love whom I please; I may love as long or as short a period as I can, to change that love every day if I please." And she made it clear, as she created a social maelstrom, that she meant sexual activity. "Yes, I *am* a free lover."

She was born in 1838 in Homer, Ohio, to a gristmill owner named Reuben Buckman Claflin and his wife Roxanna Hummel, a former housemaid. The Claflins, who lived in poverty, had many children. All the girls were beautiful, with blue eyes, fair skin and light-colored curly hair. From childhood they were aware of the world's hard ways, but they were bright and aggressive and full of the capacity for self-deception.

Roxanna, well aware of the fascination with mesmerism and hypnotism among the parlor set, was given to trances and religious ecstasies; she claimed that insistent inner voices spoke to her. At an early age Victoria had the call, too. She preached "sinners repent" to other children and soon claimed to be a clairvoyant. She had visitations from a spirit who told her, "You will know wealth and fame. You will live in a mansion in a city surrounded by ships, and you will become ruler of your people."

Buck Claflin, less spiritual than his women, burned down his gristmill in a scheme to collect the insurance. But a tar-and-feather party was promised the arsonist, so the Claflins left town in a hurry without filing a claim. They drifted about like Gypsies for years, trading livestock, living off shady card games, calling on the unknown. Virginia and her sister Tennessee were accepted throughout the Middle West as having second sight.

As "spirit callers," they were in the right place at the right time: a great wave of interest in spiritualism swept America in the 1840s, inspired by the Fox sisters of Rochester, New York, who conducted ghost rappings and presented mysteriously moving furniture. Their performances and séances in the larger cities brought in considerable money. Buck Claflin—always able to see a good thing—set up fifteen-year-old Virginia and the younger Tennessee as fortunetellers. Holding séances in boardinghouses, they managed to eat and to stay out of jail.

There is no doubt that the two young girls took their powers seriously. Notwithstanding the questionable trimmings her father may have added, Victoria herself had great faith in her own mystic powers. There was an audacity in her vitality, reinforced by her beauty, that seemed to please even the ghosts.

But there was a sensual as well as a realistic side to her, and she soon recognized her sexual potential. At the age of fifteen she married Canning Woodhull. Canning came from a good Upper New York State family; he had studied medicine and was now in Mount Gilead, Ohio, seeking to set himself up as a doctor. They met in 1853, and he asked her that first day to marry him. She said she was "elated at the promise of a little pleasure." But, according to her, three days after the wedding Canning was found drunk in a brothel. As she was to explain later, she "learned to her dismay that he was habitually unchaste and given to long fits of intoxication." He never did practice medicine and seems to have always been a complacent weakling.

After their son was born, the couple moved to California to start a new life. Victoria sold cigars, sewed, and took on bit parts as an actress, a natural career for her, since she had been role-playing all her life. Eventually, in order to support the family, she set herself up as a "spiritualist physician" and did fairly well. After a second child, a daughter, was born, she joined her family again. Reunited, all the generations of the Claflin clan moved to Cincinnati, where the police soon charged them with running a house of assignation; later, gossip insisted that Victoria had been a whore. In any case, she went on the road again, telling fortunes and holding séances.

In St. Louis she met a married man from the upper class, Colonel Harvey Blood. Kindly and well mannered, he was an idealist who also advocated free love. His philosophy seemed to dovetail with her own budding plans.

The divorces were arranged, and in 1866 a marriage license was issued to Victoria C. Woodhull and James H. Blood. There is no record of a marriage ceremony, and Victoria retained the name Woodhull.

In the mid-sixties the Claflins invaded New York, and by 1868 the names of Victoria and Tennessee were associated with that of "the richest man in the country," Commodore Vanderbilt, a widower of seventy-six. The two sisters had boldly approached the old man to bring him "spirit messages from his just dead wife." Through spirit messages Victoria advised him about the stock market, and Tennessee treated his ailment of stiffening joints with her "magnetic hands." The treatments continued into the man's bed. She called him "old boy," and he called her "my little sparrow."

Vanderbilt offered to marry Tennessee, but she rejected the offer with amusement (she was later to marry an English lord and become Lady Cook).

The spiritual advice the sisters gave on railroad stock proved to be profitable. Perhaps it was Colonel Blood, also active on the Exchange, who then suggested to Vanderbilt that the two women go into the brokerage business.

In the 1870s the sisters opened a suite of offices in the Hoffman House near Wall Street. The *Herald* ran an editorial headlined WOMEN IN WALL STREET! Other publicity on this freakish situation followed, and the connection with old Vanderbilt gave the sisters stature. They soon moved into more elaborate offices on Broad Street. The *Sun* reported NEW FUROR IN THE STREET—FIRST LEVEE AND BUSINESS RECEPTION OF VICTORIA AND TENNIE C. The *Herald* prophetically called them "The Queens of Finance."

Success came. During their reign on Wall Street they were rumored to have made half a million dollars.

Meanwhile, Victoria was living up to her idea of free love. She met a similar soul, a radical thinker from England named Stephen Pearl Andrews. He knew thirty languages, including Chinese; he introduced a system of shorthand into the United States and created a universal language called *Alwato*. He also preached a world government called Pantarchy and was called "The Pantarch" by his admirers. He seems certainly to have had great personal charm. He and Victoria, in mutual admiration, planned a social revolution. Although married, The Pantarch joined the Claflin ménage in spicy living.

Victoria issued a statement called "The First Pronunciamento" in the *Herald* in 1872, making it clear that Victoria C. Woodhull was "the most prominent representative of the unrepresented class in the

Republic. . . . I now announce myself candidate for the Presidency."
She claimed it was simply a matter of progress: "The blacks were
cattle in 1860; a negro now sits in Jeff Davis' seat in the United States
Senate. . . . As a candidate for the Presidency of the United States,
and having the means, courage, energy and strength necessary for
the race, I intend to contest it to the close." To keep up with her pace
and express her pertinacity, she had to have her own press. In May of
1870 there appeared a sixteen-page newspaper entitled *The Woodhull
& Claflin Weekly.* Against all conformity and intolerance, it carried a
simple and direct motto: "Upward and Onward."

Victoria found the existing women's rights parties too gentle and
much too man-dominated. To bring into focus the rootless drive of
women in politics, Victoria decided to create a new political party,
drawing several splinter groups of radicals and dreamers together.
The *Weekly* announced in large type: THE COSMO POLITICAL PARTY.
NOMINATION FOR PRESIDENT OF THE UNITED STATES U.S.A. IN 1872—
VICTORIA C. WOODHULL (SUBJECT TO RATIFICATION OF NATIONAL CON-
VENTION).

Victoria lectured everywhere: at the Mercantile Library, at
Cooper Union (where in only one speech Lincoln had become a
national figure), even at an opening convention of the national
association of churches, missionaries and reformers.

When the People's Party met in Apollo Hall in New York, Victoria
was at her best on the platform: "Shall we be slaves to escape
revolution? . . . Away with such weak stupidity!" She finished to a
standing ovation.

Judge Carter of Cincinnati jumped onto the platform shouting, "I
nominate Victoria C. Woodhull for President!"

Then there was a move to nominate Frederick Douglas as her
running mate, after the convention had rejected an Indian named
Spotted Tail. Douglas was nominated (he was not present and so was
unaware of the honor). Of course Victoria's name did not appear on
the national election ballots, but the nomination was a splendid
gesture for women's rights.

Meanwhile, some buried secrets of a famous man were beginning
to surface, and Victoria was to become closely involved.

In the 1870s Henry Ward Beecher was the popular and fashionable pastor of the Plymouth Church in Brooklyn. Hundreds crossed the East River on weekends in what were called "Beecher's Boats" to hear him preach against sin, slavery, pride, vanity, and spending one's capital. He was neither young nor handsome: he was approaching sixty, and he was short and fat, with long hair.

He was also what one letter writer of the times called "lickerish" (equivalent in meaning to today's "randy" or "horny"). He seduced two respectable married women in his parish—Elizabeth Tilton and Lucy Bowen—and taught them (it was later testified) the games of "nest-hiding" and "paradoxysmal kissing." When he was later confronted with these facts, Beecher said he was not the aggressor but had received letters that were "not of mere platonic affection."

Elizabeth Richards Tilton, called "Lib" by friends, was hardly the type to lure Beecher into open scandal. A small, dainty woman with big dark eyes, she had been a fan—there is no other word for it—of Henry Ward Beecher since she was ten, and she was a friend of one of his daughters. In 1855 he had read the marriage service over her and Samuel Tilton, a member of his church, and sent them off to the marriage bed with praise—"one of the finest pairs I ever married." He also got Mr. Tilton a job as editor of a religious magazine. Then one night in July 1870, Lib confessed to her husband that she and the great Christian preacher had sinned, and had been sinning for some time.

Why did she confess? She claimed that she hated the "necessary deceit of concealment." She persuaded her husband to promise not to take legal action against the great man who was "as weak in a moral sense as he was strong in his loins" (reported one western paper).

Harriet Beecher Stowe, author of the famous *Uncle Tom's Cabin,* was the sister of the popular preacher. Harriet wrote in a very mocking tone of the modern woman and her rights; she believed that the proper place for the woman was in the home. In her novel *My Wife and I* she created a character, clearly based on Victoria, called Audacia Dangereyes; this woman even asked a man up to her room for a smoke! Readers recognized the unscrupulous caricature of Victoria.

Meanwhile, a friend of Victoria who knew Elizabeth Tilton brought her story to Victoria, and on November 2, 1872, the facts of the Beecher-Tilton scandal were published in *The Weekly,* highlighted with details of the adultery. The American News Company refused to handle that issue of *The Weekly,* but there was such a rush among news dealers to pick up bundles of the papers that the police had to direct traffic around the magazine office. Beecher and his friends made a frantic effort to buy up all of the issues, but it was like trying to drive back the sea with a waving of hands.

Beecher wrote to the *Brooklyn Eagle,* damning *The Weekly*'s charges as "grossly untrue, and I stamp them in general and particular as utterly false. Respectfully, *Henry Ward Beecher.*"

Anthony Comstock, the smut hunter, got a warrant, not against Beecher but against the Claflin sisters, charging them with sending obscene matter through the mails. They were arrested and taken to the Ludlow Street jail. The scandal now took on national dimensions.

Out on bail after weeks in jail, the sisters were arrested several more times on various charges. But Victoria continued to lecture, claiming unfair treatment. And it was Beecher who now felt the wind of outrage against him, at least from some quarters.

At last Theodore Tilton accused Beecher before a church committee of "criminal seduction" of his wife's body. And on August 24, 1874, Tilton swore out a complaint in city court against the preacher for "wilful alienating and destroying Mrs. Tilton's affection for him" and demanded $100,000 for having "wholly lost the comfort, society and assistance of his said wife."

By this time, however, Mrs. Tilton had decided to deny the seduction, and Beecher made it clear to the pious that Mrs. Tilton had made the first passes: "She thrust her affections on me unsought." (He did not define how the game of "nest-hiding" was played. It has been suggested that it was played in the manner of Boccaccio's "Putting the Devil in Hell.")

The court case shocked New York and then the nation. Until World War I, churchgoing was a duty, providing social status and entertainment; it was also a constant comfort to many who were held in thrall by the great thundering preachers. Accordingly,

Beecher's being brought into court on charges of being an adulterer and the seducer of one of his own churchwomen created a wave of consternation throughout the country. The New York *Herald* sternly insisted that Dr. Beecher had a "psychological problem." The more rigid southern press went further: the Louisville *Courier-Journal* said the preacher was "a dunghill covered with flowers" (his followers had appeared in the courtroom to offer him bunches of posies).

On the other side, the *New York Times* continued to support Beecher. In one praise-filled story, no mention was made of his sins:

> *He moves his audience to tears, or brings a mirthful smile to their lips, with a power that is irresistible. His illustrations and figures are drawn chiefly from nature, and are fresh and striking. He can startle his hearers with the terrors of the law, but he prefers to preach the gospel of love. His sermons are printed weekly in the* Plymouth Pulpit, *and are read by thousands. . . .*
>
> *Mr. Beecher is young-looking and vigorous. He has the face of a great orator, and one that is well worth studying. He dresses plainly, with something of the farmer in his air, and lives simply. He is blessed with robust health, and, like his father, is fond of vigorous exercise. He has a fine farm on the Hudson, to which he repairs in the summer. Here he can indulge his love of nature without restraint.*

The trial eventually ended in a hung jury, and the members of the Plymouth Church considered their preacher completely cleared. Beecher, more popular than ever, drew thousands to hear him preach. When he traveled across the country to face packed lecture halls, he pocketed the huge fee of $1,000 a night. For a repressive section of society he became a sex symbol; for others a celebrated, pious figure of faith sorely tried, an individual who had been sent by God to show that a man can survive the blows of those who would drag him down.

Arguments about whether he was a sexual monster or if he had been betrayed and falsely branded by addled females went on in thousands of homes. For some the issue was settled three years after the trial, when Mrs. Tilton wrote a letter, reproduced in nearly every newspaper in America, in which she confessed that "the charge of adultery . . . was true." She and Beecher had indeed copulated and betrayed their marriage beds.

Such is the nature of adoration and blind faith that Elizabeth Tilton's confession did not diminish the fame or popularity of Henry Ward Beecher. His church grew more crowded with admirers when he preached the goodness and the glory, and his lectures drew bigger crowds. Many still came to see close-up the notorious male symbol of vitality.

The Beecher affair was the peak of Victoria Woodhull's life. After running for the presidency again in 1892, she moved to London, where she married a Victorian banker, John Biddulph Martin. In England she continued working for women's causes and supported Mrs. Evangeline Pankhurst in that lady's hard-fought battle for Englishwomen's right to vote. At her English country retreat she entertained the Prince of Wales at lunch, and on a trip back to the United States she interviewed President Theodore Roosevelt. In 1912 she offered a prize to the first man to fly the Atlantic, and in World War I the patriotism that led her to always keep an American flag in her dining room took more concrete form when she tried to organize a women's army in khaki.

Victoria died in 1927 at eighty-eight, having fulfilled the prophecy of more than fifty years before: "You will know great wealth and fame. . . . " Victoria's obituary in the *New York Times* made no reference to the great Beecher-Tilton scandal she had stirred up, but it did mention that Victoria Woodhull had been "a pioneer suffragist in America."

9.
It Takes All Kinds

Every kind of repression breeds a counterbalance: while women's rights advocates released the pressures of their lives by preaching, more typical turn-of-the-century women had various other ways of dealing with their emotional stress. Sometimes church duties did the trick, or growing flowers, or aiding the poor. If one could afford it, there was escape into the arts. There was also drink. A report in the *New York World* stated:

> *During the year 1869, there were 8105 women arrested for intoxication, and 3466 women for intoxication and disorderly conduct, making a total of . . . 11,571 women, in all, arrested for drunkenness.*
>
> *Wives and mothers, and even young girls, who are shamed to drink at home, go to fashionable restaurants for their liquor. Some will drink it openly, others will disguise it as much as possible. Absinthe has been introduced at these places of late years, and it is said to be very popular with the gentler sex. Those who know its effects will shudder at this. We have seen many drunken women in New York, and the majority have been well dressed and of respectable appearance. Not long since, a lady making purchases in a city store, fell helpless to the floor. The salesman, thinking she had fainted, hastened to her assistance, and found her dead drunk. . . .*

The society woman could drink in her Newport mansion, in her Lakeside-Chicago castle, at Churchill Downs; or she could become a solitary, secret New York drunk, with a butler to dispose of the empty bottles. The middle-class woman was just as addicted to alcohol, in many cases raw alcohol. Often she began the habit innocently enough by taking some nostrum, a bitter-tasting, dark brown mixture containing alcohol along with herb extracts and coloring. When addiction was solidly set, the constant need for the "medicine" became enormous. Many indulged: spinsters, housewives, maiden aunts, young brides and the elderly swallowed up millions of bottles of mixtures a year. There were many such preparations. The best known was the notorious Lydia E. Pinkham's, with a woodcut of the prim-looking, stern-faced Lydia Pinkham (of Lynn, Massachusetts) on the label.

The label boasted that the concoction

revives the drooping spirits, gives elasticity and firmness to the step, restores natural luster to the eye and plants on the pale cheek of the women the fresh roses of life's spring and early summer time.

About ninety years ago the original (Mrs.) Lydia E. Pinkham mixed up the first batch for a friend and herself. Its ostensible purpose was to treat women's "troubles," usually referred to as "the miseries": blood thinning, difficult menstrual periods, digestive disorders, and the effects of a hard-birthing. The Pinkham mixture did cheer up Mrs. Pinkham's neighbors and friends; even after the aches and pressures left, they continued to use it. Its success in the market was phenomenal.

Recommended mostly for the relief of painful menstruation and the discomforts of the change of life, the concoction appeared to ease the distress of many different symptoms. The mixture itself, "a combination of herbs," was actually made of such ingredients as licorice, chamomile, pleurisy root, Jamaica dogwood, black cohosh, life plant and dandelion root. At one time the medicine was 20 percent alcohol, but when the federal government sought to classify it as a beverage like wine and whiskey, the alcohol was cut to 13.5 percent. A single bottle could have the wallop of two or three very dry martinis. In 1925, during the mixture's heyday, annual sales were $3.8 million. Today they total around $600,000. The company has had only two unprofitable years.

10.
The Picture Lovers

The phrase "the idle rich" was in popular usage by the 1900s, as was "keeping up with the Joneses." The common impression was that society drank tea with its pinkie extended and spent a great deal of time on polo ponies or yachts, only condescending once or twice a year to pass out to the deserving poor baskets featuring naked turkeys and messages of good Christian cheer.

This was an unfair summation. Many society women did good work: they aided women's rights struggles and established public baths and settlement houses. But few ever received the credit they deserved for their good deeds.

One who did not seek recognition was Gertrude Vanderbilt, who became Mrs. Harry Payne Whitney (these fortunes merged in 1896). Harry was the catch of the social season, heir to a large portion of the Whitney millions, the fortune begun by Eli Whitney, inventor of the cotton gin. Gertrude could have easily been swept up into the social rounds of the racing stables and yachts. But she was a talented artist, serious about sculpture and art patronage. She had studied with the great Rodin, and she had the skill to transform huge blocks of marble with chisel and hammer.

In 1908 she set up an exhibition studio for artists in Greenwich Village. Visitors came to the Whitney studio, and the artists sold their work. She knew and encouraged artists of the Ash Can School: John Sloan, George Luks, Robert Henri and Childe Hassam, as well as Edward Hopper. As the Whitney studio came to be better known, it moved from place to place, always seeking larger quarters. Soon it began to take on the atmosphere of a museum dedicated to the new

American art. Gertrude began seriously to collect the works of George Bellows, Aaron Bohrod and Glenn Colman.

Soon, needing more space, she put four houses together and rebuilt the interiors, and thus was born the first version of the Whitney Museum, dedicated to the American artist. When the Armory Show of 1913 brought over the works of Cézanne, Van Gogh, Picasso, Braque, Matisse, and the Cubist painting *Nude Descending a Staircase* (which stole the show), American artists like Sloan and Kuhn found themselves ignored by collectors. It was Gertrude Whitney who gave them help and hope.

During "The Great War," as the conflict of 1914–1918 was first called, Gertrude found herself in England. Soon she was organizing her own unit of the American Ambulance Hospital. She then turned to running a medical establishment in Paris for the wounded and battle-shocked. She sailed home on the *Lusitania,* missing its sinking by a U-Boat by a season or so, and returned to Paris on the *Franconia* with loads of medical supplies.

Gertrude worked through most of the four years of war, risking her life among the German sea terrors to arrange for shipments of medical supplies to the battered Allies.

After the war ended, Gertrude stayed on in Paris for several years. She had almost no contact with the lost-generation set, for Gertrude Whitney was a serious, dedicated artist, not a bohemian. Because she was a millionairess, she was looked down upon by those expatriates who would trade their integrity for a free drink.

Gertrude's art is mostly traditional: the *Titanic Memorial Statue* is a good example of her style. She also did the *War I Memorial* that stands at Broadway and 168th Street. Moving to western themes, she made a statue of the famed American hero for the *Buffalo Bill Memorial* at Cody, Wyoming. One of Gertrude's most impressive works is the *War Memorial to the American Dead Overseas* in St. Nazaire, France.

In 1931, in order to pursue her goals of exhibiting quality American art and seeing to the welfare of the individual artists, Gertrude opened a pink marble museum (her first actual museum) on Eighth Street. The Whitney Museum encouraged the hiring of artists during the great Hoover depression and was a strong force in the Public

Works artists programs. Gertrude bought thousands of dollars' worth of their work for the museum collection. Many of these painters were later to be acclaimed as the best of the native artists.

Gertrude herself was not overlooked as a serious professional sculptor. When the Knoedler Galleries gave a one-woman show of her work, the *New York Times* sent its art critic, Edward Alden Jewell, to study what Gertrude had done for American art. He wrote, "The show just opened represents in a broad way the most notable characteristics of American sculpture and graphic art today."

The exclusive snobs at the Museum of Modern Art, which was largely controlled by the Rockefellers, kept up a jealous whisper that the Whitney touch (and that of Gertrude's assistant, Mrs. Force) could not be truly representative of all that was the art scene. Gertrude ignored them. She had done her work well. The museum contained work by Thomas Eakins, Winslow Homer, John LaFarge and Albert Ryder and others. She encouraged Walt Kuhn, John Stuart Curry and Guy Pene de Bois.

In the spring of 1942, Gertrude Whitney died, and a battle ensued over the Whitney Museum and its two thousand objects of American art. There was a time when it seemed as if it might merge with the Metropolitan Museum, but the Met was not receptive to the idea; the officials of that institution felt that the Whitney Museum attracted too radical a crowd. Finally the Whitney trustees decided to go it on their own, and they began to plan the present museum along the most radical modern lines, following a policy free from the conservatism prevailing in the art world.

Fortune magazine remarked that "Whitney women were remarkable . . . had always been as prominent, newsworthy, as active in affairs as their husbands and fathers." The statement had a condescending sound, but it was nevertheless a tribute. Gertrude Whitney, in her chosen field and with her project of a museum dedicated to modern art, may have achieved more for the public good than any of the Whitney males—including Eli himself.

A more radical spirit who was also a pioneer in bringing forward painting in America was the aggressive and free-living Marguerite

Guggenheim, better known to the art world as Peggy. Her father was Benjamin Guggenheim, who died on the *Titanic*. Her uncle, Solomon R. Guggenheim, had a museum built in New York City for his modern art collection—it is one of Frank Lloyd Wright's most original buildings.

Peggy married twice, the second time to modern surrealist painter Max Ernst. Peggy settled in a palazzo on the Grand Canal in Venice, a sort of home base and a museum visited by most of the avant-garde incrowd. Peggy was a major force in advancing the modern school of painting, helping to thrust it into world fame. She collected friendships and works from painters of the most advanced schools. While he was still an unknown, Peggy gave Jackson Pollock his first major commission for a large drip wall painting. She also published a frank and very amusing, although shocking, autobiography, *Out of My Century.*

11.
A Woman Named Addams

The wealthy's acceptance of others' poverty as "the Lord's will" long suppressed any real attempt to help the unfortunate. For example, in the middle of the nineteenth century a leading banker stated that "God has put the rich on earth to take care of the poor. There is no need for any organization."

The nation's economic progress brought misery to many. The burgeoning of industry after the Civil War, the introduction of complicated machinery which replaced field hands, the expansion of factories into settlements hacked from the wilderness, and the sprawling urban growth all combined to breed the sores that became the big-city slums. The problems were compounded by immigration, which created an oversupply of labor. As many immigrants spoke little English, they could not voice any protest. That the newcomers were inferior was a widespread impression.

Jane Addams felt differently: she believed that social responsibility was every citizen's obligation. If the government would not do so, private forces had to work to improve the lives of the neglected, the dispossessed, the exploited. She agreed with Benjamin Franklin that "Poverty often deprives a man of all spirit and virtue." She also agreed with reformer Henry George, who lectured across the land: "That amidst our highest civilization men faint and die with want is not due to the niggardliness of nature, but to the injustice of man."

Jane Addams, the daughter of a well-to-do miller, was born into upper-middle-class society in Cedarville, Illinois, in 1860. In 1882 she attended the Women's Medical College of Philadelphia, but illness forced her to drop out. Then, on a visit to England, she saw the direction her future would take. She visited Toynbee Hall in the slums of the East End and was impressed by that settlement house's work in aiding the poor with more than food. Toynbee Hall presented the message that water was for bathing, that honesty was a good policy, and that there were music and art in the world.

People who thought of Jane Addams simply as practical and logical were unaware of the inner person. As a child she had dreamed that she was the only survivor on earth and had to reinvent the wheel. Traveling around Europe after her medical school days, she began to brood about the English settlement house. According to her own account, it was at a Spanish bullfight that she suddenly decided "to rent a house in a part of the city where many primitive and actual needs are found, in which young women who had been given over too exclusively to study, might restore a balance of activity along traditional lines and learn something of life from life itself. . . . "

She was twenty-nine. With a friend, Ellen Starr, she hunted out a

Jane Addams, 1890 and 1912. The dreamer had developed an iron will.

house at Polk and Halsted streets in the worst ward of Chicago. As Jane puts it in *Twenty Years at Hull House:*

> *I was surprised and overjoyed on the very first day of our search for quarters to come upon the hospitable old house . . . built in 1856 . . . . The streets are inexpressibly dirty, the number of schools inadequate, sanitary legislation unenforced, the street lighting bad, the paving miserable and altogether lacking in the alleys and smaller streets, and the stables foul beyond description. Hundreds of houses are unconnected with the street sewer. . . . Many houses have no water supply save the faucet in the back yard, there are no fire escapes . . . wretched conditions persist. . . .*

In her work in the slums of Chicago, Jane Addams tried to express the unique worth of each human life, to teach the values of art and the making of crafts, to extend the skills of hands and fingers beyond the art of stealing. Besides providing soap, she offered many services, such as classes in the history of art and music. Most of all, she worked at counseling juvenile delinquents and helping them adjust in society.

Hull House was, she wrote, "an attempt . . . to make aesthetics a vital influence in the lives of its neighbors."

Jane Addams' strange habit of bringing poor women lectures on health and concerts of the music of Bach, Mozart and Beethoven did attract attention—and opposition from those who thought poverty a mere human triviality. Jane insisted that the city collect garbage and not let it fester in the huge wooden collection boxes of the slums. Members of the Hull House Women's Club discussed "the high death rate so persistent, [made] investigation of the condition of the alleys . . . [producing] substantiated reports of violation of the law . . . to the health department . . . one thousand and thirty-seven [violations] . . . "

Jane Addams was also antiwar. For many years she was the president of the Women's International League for Peace and Freedom, and she fought hard for the Women's Peace Party. The tragic developments of the 1914–1918 war seemed to her most pointless in what should have been a century of progress, democracy and

science. She felt that war was barbaric, youth-destroying, sense-
less. She feared "the total prevention of mutual understanding of
peoples." She attended an Emergency Peace Convention in 1915, but
prowar forces kept the convention from accomplishing very much.
The poet Vachel Lindsay called her "Our Lady of Light, our best
woman and Queen. . . . Stand now for peace though anger break
your heart. . . . " For her antiwar work, she was awarded the Nobel
Peace Prize in 1931.

Many other women lined up behind Jane Addams in both her
peace efforts and her poverty work. By the 1920s women she inspired
were making progress. Her work in the health field had resulted in
the passing of some pure-food-and-drug laws, and settlement houses
operating along the progressive lines of Hull House were becoming,
if not common, at least visible. The PTA, an outgrowth of her
women's club ideas, was flourishing. In 1919 Jane Addams celebrated
the passage of the Nineteenth Amendment; her work had helped
bring nearly ten million additional voters to the national election.

She was remembered by many, among them Upton Sinclair, who
recalls her lesser-known work with the Women's Party:

> Jane was a remarkable woman, but is now just remembered for her work
> with Hull House. She did much greater good perhaps with the American
> Women's Party. She saw it lose its punch in the 1920s when the women
> had the vote. They did carry on a bit longer, had their own building in
> Washington, D.C. Mrs. Belmont, she was married to Vanderbilt then . . .
> and she carried on, donated a lot to the cause, most of it to the Women's
> Building, and had this paper she drew up, as anti-man as men had been
> anti-women. The whole shooting match, building and all, she insisted,
> would go back to her estate if any man ever had an official position there
> or got on the payroll. Last time I saw Jane Addams she laughed at Mrs.
> Belmont's idea. You know, people thought Jane dry and humorless but
> she really had a good sense of humor. She quoted George Meredith to me:
> "Women will be the last thing civilized by man."

12.
At
Mrs. Potter Palmer's

In November 1873, just two years after the Great Chicago Fire, Potter Palmer opened the Palmer House at the corner of Monroe and State streets. It was "guaranteed fireproof" and was advertised as "The Palace Hotel of the World." The building was the fancy design of John Mill Van Osdel, done in a style "French enough" to have frightened Louis XV by its gaudy detail, but the beds were comfortable and the service good. Visitors' eyes bugged out at the splendor of the hotel, a model of masculine luxury and comfort.

Potter Palmer was not shy about speaking well of his hotel:

Most of the palaces and hotels of Europe are made up of disjointed buildings erected at various times and of mixed architecture . . . lacking in perfect form and well defined taste. The Palmer House is a realization of an era of magnificence and luxury in architecture and appointments of which the older builders knew nothing.

The other talk of the town after the Palmer House was the Potter Palmer Palace built for Mrs. Palmer; it is still standing at the corner of Lake Shore Drive and Banks Street. One guest exclaimed, "I have been in palaces of crowned heads . . . but not in Brazil, not in Russia, shall you see such taste. . . . It is a throne room fit for Liberty herself." Mrs. Potter didn't decline the role of Chicago's queen among her court, for she was creating as had Mrs. Astor, a society. This was not easy in pork-packaging, muddy, frontier Chicago. It took a woman with an iron will, a sense of style, and an air of command to influence other women to follow her example.

Mrs. Potter Palmer exemplified the society woman. From 1880 to

1910 many books were written both to help and to flatter her type. Titles such as *American Family Keepsake, How to Behave, Etiquette for Ladies* went into edition after edition—some for over fifty years.

Wrote a Mrs. Sherwood:

The well mannered and well behaved American woman . . . is the queen of the man who loves her. . . . She must be first servant-trainer . . . wife, mother, conversationalist . . . keep up with the advancing spirit of the times . . . be beautifully dressed, play the piano . . . be charitable, thoughtful . . . a student of good taste and good manners, make a home luxurious, ornamental, cheerful and restful . . . dress and entertain in perfect accord with her station, her means, and her husband's position. . . . She must steer her ship through stormy seas, and she must also learn to enjoy Wagner's music.

The *Manners Book* (1860 edition) states: "Getting married, please observe, isn't the sole object of society, however important." Other guides inform us:

You may have great trials and perplexities in your business . . . but do not therefore carry to your home a clouded brow. Your wife may have had trials which, though of less magnitude, may have been as hard to bear. A kind, consoling, and tender look, will do wonders in chasing from her brow all clouds of gloom.

The husband should never cease to be a lover, or fail in any of those delicate attentions and tender expressions of affectionate solicitude that won him his "heart's queen." It is not enough that you honor, respect and love your wife. You must put this honor, respect and love into the forms of speech and action.

As for the wife:

Never act contrary to his inclinations. Receive his wishes with attention, and execute them as quickly as possible. Apologize promptly, and in an affectionate manner, if you have allowed yourself to run into an ill-humour.

A book by a Mr. Alcott (*Young Men's Guide,* 1872 edition) was for the man who wanted a wife who could keep house. The advice is direct as to whom to marry and how to treat her:

> *Never fear the toil to her. Exercise is good for the health. Thousands of ladies who idle away the day, would give half their fortunes for that sound sleep which the stirring housewife seldom fails to enjoy. Overindulged girls play music . . . waste paper and ink in writing long half-romantic letters, or read novels. Servants! For what! To help eat, drink and sleep. . . . Look at her shoes. If they are trodden on one side, loose on the foot, or run down at the heels, it is a sign of the slipshod.*

Jane Swisshelm in *Letters to Country Girls* (1882 edition), advised against imitating the female city grasshopper:

> *Hundreds of girls in every large city, who parade the streets in feathers, flowers, silks, and laces, whose hands are soft and white as idleness can make them . . . lounge around reading novels, lisping about fashion . . . thumping some poor hired piano until it groans, and putting on airs to catch husbands.*

When Mr. Potter and Kentucky-bred Bertha Honore were married, she wore a Paris gown of white satin and rose-point lace. The bride was twenty-one and of "aristocratic stock." The guests at the June wedding numbered seven hundred of Chicago's best society. The city's soon-to-be ruling Queen Bee was off on her first flight.

The groom gave his bride his biggest asset, the Palmer House, but it soon burned down in the Great Fire. Mr. Palmer lost nearly a hundred buildings in the blaze. However, neither exhausted nor decrepit, Potter moved quickly; although he had no true collateral, an insurance company lent him $1,700,000. In 1873 the new Palmer House appeared, even grander than the first. (Costs ran so high that Palmer refused to let his bookkeeper show him the accounts.)

Mrs. Potter Palmer, of limpid sweetness and wise eyes, firmly held the reins handed her as a driver of the city's society. The new hotel finished, she arranged the marriage of her sister Ida to the son of

The Queen Bee of Chicago: the famous Mrs. Potter Palmer.

President Grant, Frederick Dent Grant. He was a man whose entire life consisted of being the general's son, but he was the catch of the season, and the general and his wife came to the wedding. Mr. Palmer looked dignified in a gray topper and gray gloves, sporting one huge pearl on a gray cravat. Mrs. Palmer wore a fortune in diamonds and pearls. Her gray flared gown was set off by Chinese red trimming, and she wore pink tea roses in her hair. The Palmers brought to the wedding their firstborn, little Honore, almost eight months old; he watched the event from a satin pillow.

At her parties Mrs. Palmer was ravishing, with her "stunning carriage, the smooth pink and white skin, the perfect teeth, wonderful hair . . . " (newspaper report). Her formal dinners for fifty saw her wearing her dog collar of 7 huge diamonds and 268 pearls. She received her guests standing before her collection of Corots, Degases, Monets and other paintings. An early buyer of French Impressionism, she had enough Monets to panel her ballroom nearly solid.

When he was grown, Mrs. Palmer put forward their son Honore for the post of alderman for the Twenty-first Ward. She had him photographed at the Palmer House wearing a waiter's uniform and carrying a tray. All the saloon and restaurant workers in his district cheered their fellow worker. Four hundred of them were invited to the Palmer castle for music, drink and food, and Mrs. Palmer shook every rough red hand. Honore was elected twice; he offended no one and sponsored no great reforms.

His mother once hired the Russian ballet for a reception she gave for Honore and his wife in Paris. She gave numerous charity balls in Chicago, and a *Tribune* reporter once wrote, "What rich city of the antique world . . . could have shown an assemblage of burghers rivaling in gold power and gold necromancy, the achievements of these decorous merchants?"

Mrs. Palmer favored women's rights, but added, "One hears so much about the new woman, that one is in danger of being bored by her unless she arrives quickly." She once wrote, "The fact of sex in women, instead of being fixed and unalterable, seems to have been a variable condition." In the matter of dress she was ahead of her era.

She said to women, "The more you put on, sometimes, the worse you look, and the more you take off, the better you look."

When Mrs. Palmer discovered that a brewery was using her regal photograph on popular saloon calendars she protested violently, but she found that there was no statute in the state against the use of her name and face. Commenting on her protests, the *Western Brewer,* bible of the beer set, wrote that Mrs. Palmer was not a private citizen, and her face and name were a national public resource. "Greatness," it concluded, "is a death to privacy."

13.
Nellie Bly:
Do or Die

Even in the last decades of the nineteenth century, when there was much hope that the twentieth century would bring a new era of great changes, women were ridiculed if they moved into two of the areas believed best handled by men: journalism and world traveling. As shown by the popular play *The Front Page,* in the 1920s reporters were supposed to be sloppy, hard-drinking men, and the few women who were in journalism were called "sob sisters." As for women as world travelers, society decreed that no woman should travel alone—she should wait until she was married and had a husband to face the evils and problems of strange places. Victorian spinsters who went to China or sought out Arab tents were cartooned as misfits better lost in those far places.

In 1890 much of this was changed by a determined woman of twenty-three who worked for the *New York World.* She was born Elizabeth Cochran in 1867, in a town named for her forefathers, Cochran's Mill, Pennsylvania (she later added an *e* to Cochran). However, she was known worldwide as Nellie Bly, the woman who beat the record of going around the world in eighty days set by Jules Verne's fictional Phineas Fogg.

She was a puny baby and a delicate, frail child; it was predicted that she "wasn't long for this world." Sent away to school, Elizabeth had to return home because of her health.

A small, slim, determined person, she refused to be pampered. She became a tomboy (a term used for any girl who handled a tennis racket with extra vigor, climbed trees, or moved about unhampered by heavy corsets under her skirts). Elizabeth had athletic brothers who helped toughen her. Because of her charm and pert beauty, the town beaux were soon coming around to the Cochran front porch to sit in the family's swing with her.

However, she had bigger plans than settling down to the life of a homemaker. She dreamed of knights and Dumas heroes; and she saw herself as the heroine in all sorts of fantastic adventures. She put some of these dreams into her early stories.

When her father died and the family was faced with grinding poverty, she persuaded them to move to Pittsburgh, resolving to support them "as a writer." Rejection slips piled up, yet she was determined to make a career as a writer. The local newspapers' editors, however, merely smiled at her offers to "just try her."

About this time, the editor of the *Pittsburgh Dispatch* published an article entitled "What Girls Are Good For" which insisted that they were to be kept in their place—at home. There had been some talk about actually hiring women to work as equals in shops and offices alongside high-collared males; the editor was firmly against that idea.

Elizabeth, outraged by the story and its author's attitude, dashed off a peppery letter but did not sign it. In the letter she firmly advocated for all women the right to choose their spots in the world, to be equal with men, to live their lives free of slavery to the home, and especially to be creative and productive.

The staff of the paper was impressed by the letter, even to the chauvinistic editor, George A. Madden. Although Madden might want women kept in their place, he was a good enough newspaperman to see that this letter would attract a great deal of attention and sell his newspapers. He discovered Elizabeth's identity and cautiously offered her the opportunity to do some short pieces on the situation of women around Pittsburgh. Her material proved to be well written and to the point. In a few weeks she had a full-time post on the *Dispatch,* and Madden, making the best of a situation not to his liking, gave her the name "Nellie Bly."

In the predominantly male city room, Elizabeth became an investigative reporter of vigor and skill. She exposed crimes against children, shopgirls and slum wives—the rejected, dispossessed and abused female world. Women had few rights in that age of dreadful, unregulated working conditions, when Pittsburgh never saw the sky through the hell its steel mills created for those who served the expanding nation's need for iron and steel.

Nellie Bly hit hard in her stories. She exposed the abuse of immigrant women by their men, as well as the widespread existence of decaying housing where children were bitten by rats. She investigated conditions of divorced women, unmarried pregnant girls, and working women dying of tuberculosis in filthy factories. Posing as a shopgirl or as a hungry mother, she visited the depraved parts of the city where prostitutes dying of disease were abused by their pimps and often murdered. In order to gather facts firsthand, she went far afield at times; once she even risked her life in women's prisons in Mexico.

Her series attracted the attention of the muckraking *New York World,* then one of the great reformist newspapers of the nation. Offered a position, she accepted, and she again found herself in the midst of an unfriendly male staff.

Nellie, however, had been through such hard times before, and she quickly became one of the top social investigation reporters of New York City. No hospital's unsanitary horror was safe from her prying eyes and exposure in her sensational prose. She fought the epidemics of tuberculosis, malaria and diphtheria that were brought on by rotting tenements, often owned by the Astors, Vanderbilts or uptown churches. She charted the crimes of Tammany Hall and exposed the corruption of city politicians. She revealed the outrageous buying of the state legislature by lobbyists for industry and the gambling, coal, whiskey, gas and trolley interests. Elizabeth even committed herself as a patient to the insane asylum on Blackwell's Island for ten days. She later wrote that she came close to losing her own mind there, as she lived in filth, a victim of cruel official indifference to the condition of mad women and girls.

The horrors she saw and experienced during these years of exposing the dreadful conditions of women in late-nineteenth-century America drove her to seek out a more romantic adventure in journalism. She suggested to her editor that she try to beat the fictional record of Jules Verne's hero, Phineas Fogg, who had traveled around the world in less than eighty days.

Her editor was doubtful. Could a slim little woman even equal that record? Alone? She insisted that she could. On November 14, 1889, with great fanfare, she sailed from Jersey City at 9:40 A.M. (plus six seconds).

Nellie Bly's 1889 trip around the world received newspaper coverage wherever Nellie traveled.

Author's collection

When she could, she sent back cables from Europe and the Middle East. People followed her progress by sticking pins on maps as she moved ever eastward. She traveled by train, ship and coach. At times she disappeared and was not heard from for days.

On January 7, 1890, she was in Yokohama boarding the steamship *Oceanic* to cross the Pacific. The ship put up a poster: FOR NELLIE BLY WE'LL WIN OR DIE.

Sixty-three days after Nellie started, her ship docked on the West Coast of America, having successfully navigated through savage storms at sea. Then it was discovered that it had left its Bill of Health behind in Yokohama. Everyone was to be held in quarantine for two weeks until another ship could bring that health clearance, for the plague was raging in Asia.

Nellie vowed that she'd jump overboard if they didn't let her leave. Finally she was permitted to board a tugboat for shore. Next she ran into blizzards on a train going east. Then she was involved in a minor train accident: in New Mexico a bridge under repair nearly dropped the train into a canyon.

As she passed through Colorado and Kansas, the suffragettes packed the depots to cheer Nellie in the name of American womanhood. There were calls for her to run for public office, although women still lacked the vote and the right to seek election.

Nellie arrived in Jersey City on January 25, 1890, at 3:41 P.M.; she had completed her journey. Tanned and weathered, carrying a small satchel and waving her ghillie travel cap, she had beat the Verne record. Her time: 72 days, 6 hours, 11 minutes.

Elizabeth remained a reformer and an investigator all her life, touring and giving lectures. She married a rich industrialist, Robert M. Seaman. Although he was fifty years older than she, their marriage appears to have been successful. After her husband's death, wily lawyers and dishonest employees of her husband's company carried off its assets. In time, she went to work for the *New York Journal* to support herself. Her last printed story was rather grotesque. She covered a legal hanging in a prison. Nellie offered the condemned man a last cigarette, which he smoked on his way to the gallows.

In 1922 she died of pneumonia at age fifty-six. Her great efforts at reform were virtually forgotten. Some remembered her as the girl who had raced around the world as a newspaper stunt. However, her old newspaper, the *Journal,* wrote: "She was considered the best reporter in America."

Years later, recalling her once great fame, a news writer said of the youthful Elizabeth:

She was poised to become the Jane Addams of Park Row, the Susan B. Anthony of the city room, Carrie Nation with printer's ink in her blood. And for a generation of Americans, her name was to be as famous as any of them.

14.
The Firebrand

Emma Goldman was born into an orthodox Jewish family in Kovno, Lithuania, in 1869. As a Jew living under Russian domination in Eastern Europe, she was a second-class citizen amidst a bigoted population, subject to the threats of pogroms and the fear of rape and even death. The brutal methods of the Tzar and the anti-Semitism of the state church were things Emma was never to forget.

In 1886, at seventeen already a boldly adventurous rebel, she and a sister came to America. They found dismal work in a Rochester, New York, clothing factory at a wage of $2.50 a week. The long grinding hours, along with the contempt of the factory system for its women workers, turned Emma into an anarchist ("a person who flouts or ignores established rules, order, duties, social behavior, seeking to exist free of governments, restraints on normal freedoms by establishments").

By 1889 she had moved to New York City. There she vocalized her beliefs and soon became editor of the anarchist magazine *Mother Earth*. She advocated free love and birth control. She also lectured on the newer works of Ibsen, Chekhov, Strindberg and others who were producing dramas exposing women's problems. From time to time she was arrested for making public her views on various subjects, but nothing could keep Emma from expressing her opinion. At one lecture she insisted, "Women, keep your minds open, your wombs closed."

Addressing an open-air meeting in Union Square, she said, "It's your sacred right to steal bread if you are starving!"

For that statement she served a year in jail.

One who heard her often in those pre–World War I years was

"Red Emma" Goldman, who
believed in sexual freedom.

Wurdemann Collection

Roger Baldwin, who was to devote his life to the encouragement of
civil liberties, including legal protection for the poor. He said:

> *Emma was the eye-opener of my life. Never before had I heard such*
> *social passion, such courageous exposure of basic evils, such electric power*
> *behind words, such a sweeping challenge to all values I had been taught*
> *to hold highest. From that day forward I was her admirer.*

Accompanying her on some of her trips was a social rebel named
Alexander Berkman whom she had met in New York and who
became her lifelong companion. Early in the century he stabbed (but
did not kill) the steel magnate Henry Frick during a great steel strike
in Pittsburgh. For this crime he served fourteen years in prison. He
and Emma were reunited after his release, and they set out together
to preach publicly that Americans should avoid the draft. They
viewed World War I as "an imperialist war" and Woodrow Wilson as
an idealistic dupe of the Allies. They were arrested for attacking the
American war effort ("to make the world safe for Democracy") and
served two years in prison.

In 1919 they were both deported to Russia in the Great Red Scare,
a program that, on the flimsiest pretexts, shipped out thousands of
Americans not born in the United States.

She was called "Red Emma," but she was actually not a follower of Marx, Lenin or Trotsky.

Max Yuron, an old socialist union organizer, remembers her as "a womanly woman":

She was universal, like rain water. A free soul. Never mind the "free love" jabber. She had dropped away long ago from any idea of ritual Judaism, a mess of ghetto acceptance of the Lord's wrath. Emma had embraced the truth that a woman, women, are produced by nature to be free of dogma, free of master states and their little moralities. But Emma in person? She was a marvelous cook. When times were hard she would open a restaurant. She could cook. I remember a place of hers, downtown New York. She and Berkman [were] like an old married couple. She was always equal she would say and her arguments had as much right to be heard as any man's. As a speaker she was logical, reasonable—if you agreed with her.

Did she have any high hopes for the Soviet Union? Yes, in the days Leon Trotsky was creating the Red Army, fighting reactionary pogromists on 40 fronts. You know the United States had an expeditionary force in Siberia? Oh yes, fighting on the side of the White terrorists. Yes, Emma had hopes for Russia; a head full of ideals. But in the end the evil of the Soviet bureaucracy caused her to speak out. Where, she asked, was the freedom; why was there torture and official mass murder? What about the rights of women? She talks, and how she could talk, against the triumph of the monolithic state and the rise to complete power of the party elitism to crush the workers and peasants.

So the bastards deported her and Alexander; that was before Stalin was shooting everybody in sight.

Her ideas on sexual freedom, women's rights in politics are accepted. She used to say in Stelton, New Jersey, over a glass of tea, "Fellow human beings, don't despair; they'll come round to our way of thinking some day. The human spirit wears out the bonds and ropes they tie us up with. The human outcry for a better, more decent world, that cry, you can't stop up your ears against it forever.

But that day, that time, did not come for Emma. She talked and she lectured. Eventually she settled in Canada, but she never lost her love for America; in 1934 she asked to be permitted in if only for ninety days. She raised funds to fight Franco during the Spanish Civil War. She pictured the horrors that would be brought on by the rise of Hitler. She spoke out against what was taking place in Stalin's Russia and in the Third Reich: "You are still free in America. No spies enter your homes for incriminating documents. No legalized assassins shoot you down in the streets."

But she and Berkman were getting old, and he was ill. In 1936 he committed suicide. And she mourned this man, so important to her life. As her depression over his loss grew, her own heart began to give out. A stroke killed her in Toronto, Canada, in 1940. The United States government permitted Emma Goldman's body to be buried in Chicago.

15.
Exorcising
the Curse on Eve

There is an impression that Margaret Sanger's work is all done and she belongs to history. Actually what she stood for and fought for is still only partly accomplished. There is still much to be done in what she began.

Eleanor Roosevelt

Early in the twentieth century Margaret Higgins Sanger was preaching birth control when the majority of respectable people still held religious opinions against it. Margaret, a practical nurse, was greatly influenced by the horrors resulting from parents' producing unwanted children. Her philosophical influences were the ideas of Havelock Ellis, who broke the silence on sexual matters in the 1890s with his *Studies in the Psychology of Sex* (and was threatened with jail for it), and the author H. G. Wells, an early advocate of sexual freedom and a student of the prevailing restrictions of marriage (including his own).

Margaret was born in 1883. Her father, an Irish stonemason, admired and supported both the reformer Henry George, the radical Single Taxer, and the agnostic Colonel Bob Ingersoll, who preached freedom from dogma and also freedom from its bigots. Under her father's guidance, she grew up with the knowledge that one had to hammer away with one's ideas in order to get anything done. She was not impressive in size, but because of her striking red-brown hair and her grim determination to have her say, she was an impressive person. Her husband, who was a socialist and an architect, fought disease-breeding tenements, as well as outdated Roman-styled public buildings. Together the young couple publicized new ideas and attacked old myths. Margaret was a vocal and earnest advocate of pacifism and women's rights, and she was critical of the overwhelming red tape of the government and its lack of concern for public welfare and health.

She advocated the control of population in order to unburden the poor of large families who could not be housed, clothed or educated properly. This idea brought her at last to a belief in the value of birth control. Some newspapers mocked her as the "First Lady of Contraception," but the fact that large families living on the poverty level needed her help was more important to Margaret. Their conditions hadn't changed much since an official report issued in the days of Victoria Woodhull:

The most wretched tenement houses are to be found. . . . The stairways are rickety and groan and tremble beneath your tread. The entries are dark and foul. . . . Every room is crowded with people. Sometimes as many as a dozen are packed into a single apartment. Decency and morality soon fade away here. Drunkenness is the general rule. . . . Thousands of children are born here every year, and thousands happily die in the first few months of infancy. Those who survive rarely see the sun until they are able to crawl out into the streets. Both old and young die at a fearful rate. They inhale disease with every breath.

The exact number of vagrant and destitute children to be found . . . is not known. There are thousands, however. . . . They do not attend the public schools, for they are too dirty and ragged. . . . Their parents are always poor, and unable to keep them in comfort. Too frequently they are drunken brutes, and then the life of the little one is simply miserable. In the morning the child is thrust out of its terrible home to pick rags, bones, cinders, or anything that can be used or sold, or to beg or steal. . . . They are disgustingly dirty. . . . The majority are old looking and ugly, but a few have bright, intelligent faces. From the time they are capable of receiving impressions, they are thrown into constant contact with vice and crime. They grow up to acquire surely and steadily the ways of their elders.

Margaret Sanger saw that what she preached had to have social and political roots. The world was already finding it hard to feed millions of people; yearly famine stalked China and parts of Africa. The slums of great cities, from the East Side of New York to White Chapel to Bombay and Singapore, were packed with hopeless millions who would never get a chance to rise above the poverty level, where the infant mortality rate was shocking. She agreed with her friend Bernard Shaw: "Don't pity the poor, abolish them." Shaw felt that a social system like his Fabian Society—the group which, in time, became the present Labour Party in England—would eventually do away with the poor, but Margaret believed that direct birth control would be more practical. With the elimination of unwanted and inadvisable pregnancies, those children that were planned would have a better chance of education and jobs and, as a result, more hope for the future.

Those who believed in unlimited breeding called Margaret a preacher for "race suicide." But, as a trained nurse dedicated to treating women's illnesses and doing maternity work, she knew, better than her detractors did, the physical horrors and the mental breakdowns that resulted from overlarge families penned up in the cold-water flats of the underprivileged. The use of women's bodies as breeding machines was both damaging and degrading. Also, as economic problems developed, men turned into brutes or drunkards, unable to support large broods of children. Clinics were filled with suicidal women.

Society looked the other way. While publicly they fought Margaret's efforts, privately the middle class practiced birth control with douching, condoms and suppositories. Although there were doctors willing to perform abortions for the rich, middle-class women went furtively to secret places to get those illegal operations from unskilled, unsanitary hands; very often painful deaths occurred from blood poisoning. The few contraceptives that were available under the drugstore counter were often not trustworthy. Public information hardly existed on this subject, so the poor, the vast slum army, were kept ignorant of what could be had. A "macho" situation also existed among them, a kind of folk tradition that a male worker had to prove his vitality and virility by keeping his wife pregnant (as Margaret discovered through interviews).

The poor in the cities in the first half of this century were, for the most part, Catholic. The Church, of course, was rigidly against contraceptives and saw sex only as a means of reproduction. Priests and nuns declared that women like Margaret Sanger were "tools of the Devil."

Margaret saw that many husbands were brutes in their sexual demands, even if they were aware that another mouth to feed and the proper raising of another child were beyond their resources. Nor was there any respect for women's rights to their own bodies; their desire to have or not to have a child was usually ignored. Frequently, if the woman protested, she was beaten or subjected to other forms of sadism.

Margaret Sanger did not fight alone; she had support from many rich women who aided her with funds and printed information. But sending "obscene" matter (which included birth control information) through the mails had been against federal laws since the 1870s. Fanatical opponents watched what Margaret's group mailed out and raised howling protests against even the most factual material. Margaret Sanger was frequently in jail or fighting in courtrooms before intolerant judges. She tried, often in vain, to get her views published in indifferent media that depended on pleasing the big advertisers, who were often against any views which they themselves did not hold. When the *New York Call* did print her frank series on sexual education, "What Every Mother Should Know," and the even more "shocking" series "What Every Girl Should Know," the newspaper had legal troubles because it had printed such words as *gonorrhea* and *syphilis*.

What enraged many was Margaret's insistence that a reasonable method of birth control would make sexual pleasures more enjoyable, that women's rights would seem clearer to well-adjusted sexual partners, and that with public encouragement men could be reasoned with to take precautions against impregnating their partners. It was particularly the idea that sex without hope of issue was pleasurable and normal that raised great outcries. The curse of Eve was often cited: "Woman may be said to be an inferior" (Aristotle); "The judgment of God be upon your sex . . . you are the gateway of the Devil. Nothing is as much to be shunned as sex relations" (St. Augustine).

In 1914 Margaret began to publish a magazine called *The Woman Rebel*. Its slogan was "No gods, no masters." Margaret was indicted for "obscenities" in her magazine; her husband was arrested for selling a copy of it.

(Eventually the case against her magazine was declared *nolle prosequi* [no case].)

In 1916, in Brooklyn's Brownsville section, she opened the first birth control clinic in America. Here she proceeded to supply education, information and the Mensigna pessary, a contraceptive Margaret had been impressed with on a recent visit to Holland. The city, ruled by Tammany, which in turn was under the thumb of the local cardinal, sent the police to raid the clinic. Margaret was jailed more than once, and her sister nearly died in a hunger strike on behalf of birth control. Margaret did not care to whom she preached her cause as long as she was heard. She even spoke to the ladies of the Ku Klux Klan. Still, the press would feature her only in some sensational jailing or court battle.

Margaret strove for birth control for over four decades—until she died in 1966. As Mrs. Roosevelt said, her cause for sexual freedom and equality of the sexes is far from won.

A woman who worked with Margaret Sanger states:

The fanatics' creed still controls. It still battles abortion, even if it is now legal, and still keeps the Women's Rights Amendment from passage. Pressures from strange places work on Congressmen and Senators who bury bills, even recall legislation already passed. All this is done under slogans of Right to Live, Anti-communism, No Welfare Payments for Abortion for the Poor. Prejudices become respectable, women's rights are called "destroyers of homes and marriages."

Margaret Sanger did her work well, fought the secrecy of sex; the uninformed bride horrified on her wedding night is rare today. Sex education exists in most schools, fought as it is by anti-information groups with their picket lines and biased view of reality. Our gospel has been accepted in our more permissive times; unsanctioned sex is not today

the road to hellfire and damnation, and no longer accepted is the idea
that sanctified sexual relationships are always splendid and lead to
happiness. Many now agree that children planned for and educated
properly make for happier families and a stronger economy—as Margaret wrote—if only in producing better stock, and in less number.
Cohabitation is as rewarding in a culture as sex just for the producing of
offspring. And because of Margaret Sanger, simple, safe, adequate
contraceptive methods do exist.

16.
Helena the Great and Madame Demorest

Women have always had ideas about improving their appearance; excavations in ancient Crete, Egypt and Persia have revealed containers of dried face colors and other objects relating to cosmetics buried with their users. In Western culture, however, cosmetics were frowned upon until very modern times. Mrs. Trollope did note that American women used to dash a little powdered corn starch on their faces to cover their weathered complexions, but those who used other methods to heighten color were considered prostitutes or actresses (the boundaries between these two classes, many insisted, were not distinct).

Was it our Puritan beginnings or the natural conditioning of a pioneer society that caused us to look down upon ornamentation of the human body? In 1674 William Wycherley wrote of a woman who used "cosmetics": "She looked like an old coach newly painted." An even older text stated that "A painted face is the Devil's looking glass," and, to show that honorable women didn't need it, added, "Painting is the enemy of blushing, which is virtue's color." The idea that cosmetics were for "fast women" lasted well into the twentieth century. Respectable women restricted themselves to a little rice powder.

It was the French who saw that the use of cosmetics added a glow to nature. Perhaps English women, with their "milkmaid's complexion," felt they did not need to adorn what was already perfect. But Pierre Antoine Berryer, in the nineteenth century, believed that "There are no ugly women; there are only women who do not use cosmetics."

The natural use of cosmetics by nearly every woman came late to

America. The first beauty salon in the Western Hemisphere did not open until 1908. That beginning of elegance was the work of Helena Rubinstein. She was also one of the creators of the huge modern industry, with its thousands of products and its giant advertising budgets for unguents, creams, lotions, nail enamels, false eyelashes.

She changed the appearance of women by revealing the secrets of pastel powdering, coloring, hair tinting ("Never say dye, better instead bite the tongue," she insisted). She encouraged women to believe that they could change their appearances for the better. (She herself was only four feet ten, but she "looked tall.")

Helena Rubinstein was born in Poland in 1872 of Jewish parents. Even as a girl she was convinced that with her high spirits and intellect she could impress herself on the world. When she was an effervescent teenager, her family forbade her to marry a student whom she loved. Outraged, she packed up a dozen jars of her mother's skin cream—a "face food," as she was to call it later—and made her way to wild Australia, where she had relatives. The impression that Madame, as she preferred to be called, mixed her cosmetic potions is not true. The face cream she took to Down Under, the "Creme Valaze," was the concoction of a Hungarian friend of the family, a Dr. Lykusky.

Helena had a hard time of it at first. She worked for a short time as a waitress at the Café Dore, where she soon learned English. But when many wondered how Helena's skin remained so smooth and soft in the dry Australian climate, out came Dr. Lykusky's cream, and she was soon in business in Melbourne on a borrowed thousand dollars. She wrote to the doctor to ship her gallons more of his mixture. She stated later, "I never regretted it."

Helena bought bottles, printed labels, and was soon a success. She sold the cream and gave lessons in skin care to sheep-ranch wives as well as to city women. As no such thing as a beauty salon existed, she recognized the merit of combining treatment and sales. She began to concoct other items, although she had no true knowledge of chemistry or training for lab work. She brought Dr. Lykusky and his two sisters, Manka and Ceska, to Australia to help in her lab kitchen and with sales. The press interviewed her at her Maison de Beauté Valaze, and soon a large part of the feminine population was writing her for advice and for the cream (made of mineral oil, ceresine wax and sesame). She offered to return the people's money if they were not satisfied, and "Only one capricious person asked for her money back." From the first Helena maintained a sublime imperturbability.

By 1904 she was advertising, *"Mlle. Helena Rubinstein . . . announces the launching of Valaze Russian Skin Food by Doctor Lykusky, the celebrated skin specialist."* Later both the doctor and the claims of the cream's being Russian were dropped. It was Helena all the way. The name *Valaze,* used on all her early products and salons, never has been explained.

Why did she leave Australia? Even Patrick O'Higgins, her assistant for many years, did not fully explain it in his fine story of her life, *Madame.* Madame talked of a suitor, Edward Titus, who was so insistent, she claimed, that she could hold him off until she could make up her mind only by going to London to open a salon. She promised, "If I was successful in London, I would then accept his proposal." She was thirty by then and aware of the intrinsic value of things. The salon was a success, and they were married.

The move was not just a romantic interlude in her life; it was the start of a cosmetic empire. Up to then women of most classes had been the victims of hairdressers and of dangerous items often procured in little shops. Now there were home hair-curling aids, and there would soon be a string of Valaze Beauty Salons.

Helena began to expand her fame as American women visited her salons and took back her products. Madame produced two sons, the second in 1912, the year she moved to Paris to watch over her *Salon de Beauté.* She increased the number of salons and the number of products. When the Great War began, she moved the family to New York. She cited her husband as the cause of the move. "Edward was an American citizen. He insisted we go to America for the sake of our sons."

She kept her eyes open for the cosmetic needs of American women, and she soon set up her first American salon in a West Forty-ninth Street brownstone. She hardly noticed when Edward disappeared with one of her shop assistants. But husband and wife

Helena Rubinstein in the 1920s. Her dress is by the renowned designer Poiret.

were apparently reconciled from time to time, until she married the Prince Gourielli in 1938.

People who knew her best say that she was cunning, stingy, clever, a bargain hunter, one of the most successful businesswomen of her time, and an advertising genius. Certainly one could add to this that she was also a source of comfort to millions of women, for she encouraged the American woman's search for grace and beauty. Also, her salons were training grounds where plain women might try on the plumage of the bird of paradise. "I did more to keep many women sane than the psychologists."

Progress was swift. Soon there was the Rubinstein building on Fifth Avenue where several hundred people were employed. In time a factory was built on Long Island. By 1950 the Rubinstein-America setup was grossing $25 million a year; when the company went public, Helena held 52 percent of the shares. Then the company expanded abroad. The Far East was made into an empire of scents, oils and by-products. It was estimated that Helena personally was worth $150 million by the time she died in 1965, at more than ninety years of age.

Helena Rubinstein had rivals by then: Elizabeth Arden was "The Other One"; Charles Revson was "The Nail Man," whom she accused of copying her products. But bejeweled and regal, Helena was an exhilarating sufficiency unto herself. She once told a young female reporter who had questioned the high price of some beauty item:

> *Look, my girl, you can say maybe it's four cents' worth of lard and smells in a fifteen-dollar flask. But with it is thirty—no, say forty—years of experience. In that flask is a miracle—a woman who buys it buys confidence. There is in it also poise, a knowing you're beautiful, you're desirable. Wait till you're older, you'll find I give you what nothing else can: not even fame, money, love. Helena Rubinstein gives a yourself you like.*

American women who cared about their appearance had Madame to thank. Soon the ordinary housewife could pick up Rubinstein products. Because Helena knew how to present her cosmetics as an act of acceptance of beauty, women from society leaders to high school cheerleaders bought her line.

She was a visionary who insisted that the rewards of cosmetics be experienced by every woman who owned a mirror.

While Helena Rubinstein was revolutionizing the world of cosmetics, Madame Demorest was doing the same for women's clothing through her Emporium of Fashion in New York.

Like Helena Rubinstein, Madame Demorest was a female version of the popular Horatio Alger hero who achieved material success in an expanding economy. The *Madame* was an affectation. A farm girl from Saratoga, she was an apprentice to a dressmaker and then an expert hat designer; later she manufactured corsets.

Madame Demorest began her business career with a modest shop in New York. She soon saw that the American designs with their flounces and gewgaws could be improved upon by importing fashionably designed modes from Paris. She studied the imports, measured them, and pirated them, transforming them into patterns. Consequently, as the magazine *New York Illustrated* noted, her conversions were "not only available to the wealthy and fashionable but to persons in middle life and the lowly"—this in an era when the local seamstress served most women, and the ready-to-wear industry hardly existed. Now many women could do away with visits to the local dressmaker, and of course the seamstresses themselves bought thousands of these patterns; so the good taste of Madame Demorest spread.

Madame's factory and mail-order pattern business and showroom were on Union Square, then the heart of New York. She had a grand salon where ladies could come to look over the graceful and elegant gowns and costumes made from her patterns and suited to every face and figure and all ages. On its six floors her Emporium employed over two hundred girls working on cloth and on the preparation of paper patterns. Pictures of the final garment and instructions— some in Spanish, French or German—accompanied the patterns. There seems to have been an almost modern assembly-line system of designing and cutting, and the stockrooms and storerooms were efficiently run.

Madame's husband published fashion and family magazines which featured woodcuts of stiff gentlemen and prim but proud ladies wearing what was accepted as the height of fashion. What with the workshops, the publications, and the sale of tissue-paper patterns through the mail, the team of Mr. and Mrs. Demorest dominated the field of fashion for the properly and respectably dressed woman.

Madame Demorest's thin paper patterns were an inspiration to women from the Atlantic to the Pacific; they went out to Kansas farms and to Nob Hill houses in San Francisco. From Union Square Madame Demorest tried to ship out every order the same day it was received. It was claimed that when one of the costumes caught on, she could sell nearly fifty-five thousand copies of that item. She may not have invented the pattern that made her famous, but she did exploit it to the limit.

There was also a Demorest office in Paris for European women who wanted fashionable and graceful clothing.

It is interesting that Madame's attempt to make style acceptable to middle-class women also pleased the society women who patronized the Union Square establishment. Although many society women deserted Madame Demorest when it was discovered that she employed "colored girls," they soon came back. Mrs. Astor's friends could not afford to cut off their source of fashion just to spite a minority. (Oddly enough, they did not object to black house servants, coachmen, valets or cooks.)

Madame Demorest, like other popular figures famous in her day, was honored by many, and she proudly displayed her medals and engraved parchments. Her Emporium was lauded as an "enterprising management [that] deserves great credit for the benefit they have bestowed on the cultivation of taste . . . constantly united with the aesthetic."

17.
A Woman with a Blue Flame

Sensuality was one of the gifts of some of the Queen Bees. Before World War I began, a woman of thirty-five, described by herself as "buxom, comely, muscular, and hearty," stood at the rail of an ocean liner with her young son as the ship moved toward the skyline of New York. She had lived abroad for many years. She told her son that everything worthwhile was behind them. America was all machinery and factories; it was, to her, *"ugly, ugly, ugly."*

Mabel Dodge was to found one of the most impressive New York literary and political salons of the twentieth century. She settled into a second-story apartment in a brownstone owned by a one-legged Civil War veteran, General Daniel Sickles, at Ninth Street and Fifth Avenue, near the Hotel Brevoort.

Born in 1879 to a very wealthy couple in Buffalo, New York, Mabel was raised to expect a life of luxury and attention. When she returned to America she was already on her second marriage. (Her son John was a product of her first marriage.) And the days of second husband Edwin Dodge, an architect who helped set up the apartment at 23 Fifth Avenue, were also numbered, for he failed in some mystic test her mates had to pass. For three years before settling in New York, Mabel had lived in her Villa Curonia in Florence, Italy, where she moved in a cultural circle of writers and painters, mostly Americans like herself. There was a wary friendship with Gertrude Stein, who, she noted, "had a laugh like a beefsteak." In her fractured style, Gertrude wrote *A Portrait of Mabel Dodge and The Villa Curonia* (now out of print).

Once settled in New York with a few servants, including a very proper butler, Mabel painted and papered her apartment white; in

her many-volumed autobiography, *Intimate Memories,* she mentions
that white helped her moods. She then added a white marble
fireplace, a white polar bear rug, gilded mirrors, chaises, chairs in
French blues and lemon-yellow, and pearl gray rugs. Candles flick-
ered in a white porcelain Venetian chandelier decorated with flowers
and birds.

Mabel wanted to be a stoic, to be able to face the problems of life
without showing her true emotions. A New York friend, Carl Van
Vechten, music critic and style-setter, used Mabel as the model for
the character Edith Dale in his novel *Peter Whiffle.* He described her
as "a dynamo . . . a face that could express anything, or nothing, more
easily than any I have ever seen. It is a perfect mask . . . "

Max Eastman, a writer and critic, saw her as plebeian: "Sexed all
over in a way you laugh at and like; not intellectual, insensitive." He
adds that she was "unkind, if kindness is quick sympathy," and that
she had a wish to "mate the universe with mystery in her own soil . . .
a sphinx." Mabel, after she married Edwin Dodge, saw herself as one
who wanted "to be alive like fire" and thus experimented sexually.

She was among the first in America to talk to a Freudian prac-
titioner of psychoanalysis. Therapy didn't offer her much help; she
found that having her tonsils removed supplied greater comfort. The
tonsillectomy was performed in her own bed in the apartment. To
entertain her, Edwin Dodge brought in a friend, Jo Davidson, a burly
sculptor. Davidson found the hostess appealing in her big white bed,
and sensed that here was a patron—and more. He liked the luxury of
the place, the drinks, the food, Mabel's Turkish cigarettes, and—
particularly—Mabel herself.

Davidson came again and brought Walter Lippmann, who was
just starting his career as a journalist philosopher. Lincoln Steffens
and Hutchins Hapgood of the *New York Globe,* a nonstop talker who
described himself as "a philosophical anarchist," also came.

Her salon grew, and her "evenings" became *the* place to meet
intellectuals and rebels of many kinds. It all had a new exalting flavor.
After the post-Impressionists, Fauvists, Cubists, and Futurists, the
people in the know, all agreed at Mabel's "evenings" that a show was
just what the nation needed, her salon supported the 1913 show of

modern paintings at the Sixty-ninth Street Regiment Armory. Mabel herself helped arrange the exhibition, even offering her chauffeur Albert and her own limousine (once described by a Villager as "long as a tapeworm"). Her role in introducing modern art to the average American was an important one.

Mabel knew how to run a successful salon. As she told Walter Lippmann, "I would rather be a leaf in the wind than the wind." Mabel (Edwin having departed for good) was the crowned Queen Bee of the intellectuals. She wore long white dresses with scarves of green chiffon and stood among vases of lilies, blue larkspur and snapdragons when she greeted her guests. The white walls were hung with American moderns. She saw herself made of "shy and suspicious sensibilities . . . people flowed in, I stood apart, aloof and withdrawn. . . . "

A hundred people usually gathered for one of Mabel's "evenings," and the talk was daring for that postwar time: Psychoanalysis, Sex Antagonism, Sacred Names and Scarlet Mores, Birth Control (Margaret Sanger attended), Union Organization, Revolution, Revolt of the Masses, Women's Rights, Anarchism. (It was a period when words with capital letters were popular.) Mabel announced that her "evenings" were "one stream where many currents mingle together," and added, perhaps wistfully, "for a little time."

> And life is very fair,
> In Washington Square . . .

So wrote John Reed, one of her guests. Known as "The Golden Boy" to the Villagers and as a romantic revolutionary to the radicals, he had come down from Harvard in 1910 to write and preach rebellion. He wrote short stories and articles—even for the establishment's *Saturday Evening Post.* Only twenty-six and a poet of sorts (the above quotation is from his *Day in Bohemia*), Reed saw that "reality transcended all the fine poetic inventions."

Reed was tall and handsome, with brown hair in Byronic disorder over a thinker's brow. Max Eastman thought, however, that he had "a too filled-out face that reminded me of a potato."

Reed first met Mabel not at an "evening," but in an artist's studio. Mabel was interested, as all the radicals were, in the Paterson mill strikes. When Mabel was asked where she would recommend holding a great mass meeting supporting the strikers' cause, she answered, "Why not Madison Square Garden?" John Reed whispered to her, "My name is John Reed," and to the roomful of people he shouted, "I'll do it."

The rally was a success; fifteen thousand people packed the Garden to view the Paterson pageant. It was a triumph for Mabel and for John, and they adored each other. But they had not yet made love. Mabel in her memoirs, wrote that it was she who suggested her Villa Curonia in Florence as a haven from the world. After their ship sailed, John tapped on Mabel's stateroom door. She addressed him through a crack and shook her head, "Darling, we are just on the Threshold . . . nothing is ever so wonderful as the Threshold of things, don't you *know* that?"

It was in Paris that the Threshold was passed. John whispered to her, "I thought your fire was crimson, but you burn blue in the dark."

World War I wrecked the love affair. John Reed wrote Mabel, "This is not a crusade against militarism, but a scramble for spoils. This is not our war." Mabel, however, was loyal to the Allies and returned to Fifth Avenue and a New York lover, the painter Maurice Sterns, whom she was to marry. John Reed testified before a congressional committee in Washington, "You can shoot me if you want to, and try to draft me to fight." Then, in Oregon on a visit home, he met Louise Bryant. She was already married, but they lived together in Washington Square. John went to Europe to see the war end and died of fever in Moscow.

After a short marriage to Maurice Sterns in the 1920s, Mabel Dodge left New York for Taos, New Mexico, where she married a Pueblo Indian named Tony Luhan and worked on her amazingly frank memoirs. In Taos she insisted that she was making magic to will D. H. Lawrence to come to her. "I leaped through space joining myself to the central core of Lawrence where he was. . . . " He came and she made a shrine for him.

She died at the age of eighty-three in 1962.

Library of Congress

Mabel Dodge with her Indian husband Tony Luhan, at home in Taos, New Mexico.

She belongs to our times, for all her strange moments and odd acts, as a fully free woman. It is true that she was vain and that her ego often outran her abilities, but she sought a larger dose of life. She had adaptability; she was robust, yet natural. She was an example of modern female freedom for many women in her time. The *New Yorker* summed her up as one "who was made up of vanity, willfulness (if not will), generosity (with a mean streak), intellectual curiosity, mystic nonsense, and earthy sense . . . a woman who decided to make something of herself in an age when being a woman of her class was looked upon as merely one of the decorative arts."

18.
Mary Cassatt and the Cone Sisters

As taste-makers, women did a great deal to bring the newer art forms into American view. First, they concentrated on private collections; then, man and woman being mortal, they donated their art to great museums like the Metropolitan in New York and the National Gallery in Washington, D.C. In our time, collectors such as Morgan, Frick and Guggenheim established their own museums.

When long-chinned Mary Stevenson Cassatt, aged twenty-two, went to Paris in 1866 to paint seriously, she was more provocative than lovable. A student from the Philadelphia School of Art, she had been to Paris with her family several times before. She was already an outspoken personality, and she hardened even more as she aged. But many believed that she painted the best Impressionist paintings done by an American. As one French collector put it, *Le grand peintre américain est Mary Cassatt.*"

She was born in Allegheny City, Pennsylvania, on May 22, 1844. Her family were Scotch-Irish Episcopalians with claims to French Huguenot connections. Her brother Alexander was the president of the great Pennsylvania Railroad system.

From her vantage point in Paris, Mary was instrumental in moving Impressionism across the Atlantic to the homes of the American wealthy by always insisting that visitors buy one or two.

She studied art seriously in France and showed a most charming and important picture at the fourth Impressionist show in 1879: *La Loge,* a red-haired girl in a pink gown seated in an opera box. Paul Gauguin, who liked the work, said of Mary, "Mlle Cassatt has as much charm, but she has more power." (*"Mlle Cassatt a autant de charme, mais elle a plus de force."*)

Degas was a close friend, and when he needed money she helped him. Like his, her view of the human race was critical; she found most people to be foolish or offensive.

And like Jonathan Swift, she preferred horses to human Yahoos. (This affection for animals did not extend to birds, however—their plumes decorated many of her hats.) In the summer of 1888 her love of riding nearly killed her. Degas wrote:

> Mlle. Cassatt has had a fall from a horse, broken the tibia of her right leg, dislocated her left shoulder . . . she is getting on well . . . she will be immobilized for weeks this summer, then deprived of any activity, and most surely of her passion as a horsewoman. . . . The horse most likely put a foot down a hole made by the rain.

Again in 1890 horses were bad luck for her: she was tossed from her carriage onto the stones of the Rue Pierre Charron, and "as I alighted on my forehead, I have the blackest eye . . . anyone was ever disfigured with." The carriage was splintered nearly to bits by the kicking horse, the coachman fell off his perch, and the dogs riding in the carriage were injured.

It was never easy to find out just where she stood in relationship to her native land. Yet she did write in a letter, "I am an American, definitely and frankly an American." Mary Cassatt's mother defined both her and her daughter's attitude toward Americans in Europe: "We jog along as usual and make no acquaintances among the Americans who form the colony, for as a rule they are people one wouldn't want to know at home." Seeking permanent roots, Mary moved into an apartment on the rue de Marignan which she kept until her death.

Mary was called "the painter of the modern Madonna" by the *Chicago Inter-Ocean*. In 1904 she was made a *Chevalier de la Legion d'honneur*. She had turned down such an honor earlier when the nation of Luxembourg, with typical French frugality, had offered to trade the red sliver of ribbon for one of her paintings.

About this time, Mary's family came over to tour Europe with her, bringing both a White Steamer and Mary's own Renault landaulet.

Mary began to dabble in spiritualism the way many skeptics do, but it did not affect her painting.

By 1911 she had cataracts on both eyes, but "Dr. Borsch, he is a Philadelphian," she wrote, would operate. The operations were not very successful. The war of 1914 forced her to live out the fearful times in a villa at Grasse. By then, Europe, through her efforts, was aware that an American and a woman could be a major artist.

In 1917 Degas died. "My oldest friend. I see no one to replace him." The times were out of joint for her. She had raged when one of her paintings was sent by a dealer to the famous 1913 Armory show in New York. She despised her great contemporaries. Matisse's work she found "extremely feeble . . . commonplace." Scorn was all the Cubists were worth. Monet's remarkable paintings of waterlilies looked to her "like glorified wallpaper." In 1908 she had been lured into meeting Gertrude Stein at the Rue de Fleurus. She looked over the Cézannes, Picassos and Matisses, and said to the woman who had brought her there, "I have *never* in my life seen so many dreadful paintings in one place! I have never seen so many dreadful people gathered together and I want to be taken home at once." Out she marched to her car waiting at the curb.

She had little respect for Henry James and detested Edith Wharton, who she felt was "a bad writer." There was no pleasing Mary. Perhaps the physical suffering of the eye operations that went on in series and did not improve her sight made life unendurable. She had no students and was not friendly to other female painters.

She died in 1926, having proven herself an American painter of genius among the great French Impressionist masters. Today her paintings hang in nearly every major museum in the world.

It is a long leap from the stern Yankee traditions of Mary Cassatt to the Parisian world of Dr. Claribel Cone and her sister Etta. But these eccentric Jewish ladies were also responsible for introducing new and different works by artists previously unknown in America.

Doctor Claribel Cone was born in Tennessee in 1864 and arrived in Baltimore at the age of six, a strong-minded, spoiled, bright child. Growing up to be massive, she decided to compete in a man's world by becoming a doctor. The only medical school south of Washington that would take female students was the Baltimore Women's Medical College. Claribel was graduated from there in 1890.

Her opulent bourgeois family owned cotton mills, and so Doctor Claribel was not pushed into general practice. She preferred pathology and studied under the renowned Doctor William Henry Welch at Johns Hopkins; then she worked with Metchnikov in Paris and with Ehrlich at Frankfurt. She also published a few articles on gross and cellular pathology and physiology.

In 1905 Claribel and her sister Etta (born in 1866) traveled to Paris on the first of their thirty visits. These unmarried fortyish women went to visit their friend and distant cousin Gertrude Stein. Gertrude's oldest brother, Michael, introduced the Cones to Matisse. It was Etta who in 1906 bought the Matisse painting *The Yellow Jug,* the first of the sixty-six Matisses the sisters were to leave to the Baltimore Museum of Fine Art.

Etta, the younger of the two, was the mild-mannered one. People remember her calming Claribel during her rages. She had a great love for cooking and would often reward an artist by baking him a cake. (Matisse preferred chocolate for his birthday.) Gertrude, who ruled friendships with an iron hand, called Etta "a distant connection" and said Etta found Picasso "appalling but romantic." Etta did buy Picasso drawings at his studio; she spent about a hundred francs a visit, or twenty dollars at the Edwardian rate of exchange. She preferred the sweet and pretty Picassos and Matisses to the artists' more experimental works.

Etta had no profession, so she began to help Gertrude by typing the manuscript for a book called *Three Lives.* It was typical of her that, feeling that she hadn't been given permission to read it, she typed it one letter at a time to avoid catching the meaning of the text. She once said to Alice Toklas, "I can forgive but never forget." Alice, who always knew an opening when she was given one, answered, "I can forget but never forgive."

Doctor Claribel Cone, who had a deep ram's horn of a voice, enjoyed reading Gertrude's more exotic experimental prose aloud.

She would read, then whisper to a baffled guest, "I don't really understand any of it." Both sisters at this time were enthusiastic members of the Stein "clan."

Doctor Claribel, with an insatiable appetite for glitter, was demanding of life, and Etta meekly followed suit. Claribel liked good food, comfortable rooms and enormous beds. In Paris she could demand and command like a field marshal. When she and Etta traveled, she would howl if the room was not totally comfortable. When Etta pleaded, "But, Claribel, it's only for one night," Claribel would shake her head as if she were going to the rack. "*One* night is as important as any other night in my life. I *demand* to be comfortable!"

Picasso called the two formidable sisters "The Etta Cones." He did a stern, solid two-sided drawing of Doctor Claribel. Upon its completion, Doctor Claribel pulled up her skirts and petticoats to reveal a stout, oaklike leg, and from a secret pocket among the lacy froufrou, she produced a thousand-franc note which she handed to the artist, "In payment, *cher maître.*" The picture is now in the Baltimore Museum of Art.

Picasso told the Cones he was a fan of American comic strips, or "funny papers," as they were then called. His favorite was "The Katzenjammer Kids," which told the wild, slapstick adventures of a shipwrecked German family marooned on a tropical island: Mama, Der Captain, Der Inspector, two bad boys—Hans *und* Fritz. To his delight the Cone sisters kept Picasso supplied with bundles of these colored comic cartoons.

Etta was given to baggy, comfortable clothes, but Doctor Claribel preferred fantastic costumes. A theater lover—mostly for display of herself—she would appear hung with ornaments from the East, her large breasts festooned with Renaissance jewelry, her built-up coiffure stuck with geisha pins. To this were often added colorful shawls from Spain and capes made from Chinese mandarin or Japanese Kabuki robes. There were rumors that she smoked cigars in private.

Back home again with their antiques, peculiar fashions, and art, the sisters would settle into their overcrowded Eutaw Street apartment in Baltimore to plan other trips. Besides the great paintings, they bought glorious junk. They were the eager victims of many shady dealers; they purchased sets of furniture that were labeled "Queene Anne" and "Renaissance"—and sometimes were. There were Oriental rugs, always described as "priceless"; primitive bronzes stood beside Persian cloth; Asian artifacts and African ritual items had their places. Doctor Claribel's passion was also on display: her collection of intricate boxes and chests.

In 1929, at sixty-five, Dr. Claribel Cone died on Eutaw Street among the paintings, the Oriental rugs, and the Renaissance furniture.

The following year Matisse came to America, bringing with him some huge murals he had painted for an eccentric Doctor Barnes, "the mad collector of art" in Merion, Pennsylvania. After a not too happy encounter with Doctor Barnes, he came on to Baltimore to visit Etta. He enjoyed seeing his work on the walls of the apartment and promised to make a posthumous portrait of Doctor Claribel, which he did in 1934; he also did one of Etta in charcoal. In Etta's portrait she appears wide and aged, but serene; she is seated in a stiff-backed chair, her face solid-looking, her hair done in an old-fashioned style.

The year of this Matisse drawing was also the year Etta bought his huge work, *The Magnolia Branch*. Five feet square, it was perhaps the most important Matisse in America. Etta continued to buy a picture from the artist every year and *always* mailed him a birthday cake. She eventually published a catalog of the Matisse collection: thirty-two oils, eighteen drawings, seventy studies for the artist's Mallarmé etchings, and eighteen bronzes.

In August of 1949, twenty years after Doctor Claribel, Etta died. The Cone sisters' magnificent bequest to the Baltimore Museum of Art was impressive. Their collection of major works of art, not counting drawings and prints, included 180 items when it went as a gift to the Museum. Besides the Matisses and Picassos, the collection contained Renoirs, Van Goghs, Cézannes and Manets. At that as yet uninflated time, it was valued at three million dollars; today, in the overvalued dealer-controlled and -manipulated international art market, the collection merits that misused word *priceless*. No one

knows the millions that the 180 major masterworks of the Post-
Impressionists and School of Paris would bring at auction today.
As one magazine writer put it:

> By the time Miss Etta died, the "odd Cones" in Eutaw Street had become
> owners of one of the most fabulous private collections of modern
> paintings in existence, and once stuffy Baltimore was miraculously
> endowed with an art gold mine.

19.
Mrs. Wharton Regrets

Social history in a literary form was traditionally written by men. When women did attempt it, they took masculine pen names; for example, George Eliot and George Sand. The first modern woman novelist to step boldly forward as a critic of society used her own name, Edith Wharton.

Edith was born in 1862 in New York City, and her last name was plain Jones. Like many of her class, she had little serious education. She was taught manners and graces, but was really educated by her extensive reading. She joined New York's best society when she married Teddy Wharton, a man who never had a profession but did have a great deal of money. Edward Robbins Wharton, twelve years older than Edith, was a Harvard graduate, a fly fisherman, a figure skater, and a hunt rider. She was twenty-three when she married, an intellectual deeply embedded in the glossy, glazed society of her times. By the turn of the century the childless couple were habitual travelers across the Atlantic.

After a time, the marriage began to fail. When Edith sought out noted neurologist Weir Mitchell about her frustrations as a wife to her mentally ill husband (today medical science would treat Teddy as a man moving into a final mental breakdown), Dr. Mitchell advised her to turn to writing. It seemed a safe enough niche, so she wrote.

In 1899 she published a book of short stories. The next year, a novel entitled *The Touchstone* appeared. From then on she usually brought out a book a year, both in the United States and in England. Often they were bestsellers, and her example encouraged other women to write fiction.

Edith had sharp literary teeth—she attacked upper-class Ameri-

Ross Collection

Edith Wharton, grande dame of American writers, in full social regalia.

can society with ironic fury and fine style. Her friend Henry James called her "the angel of devastation." Walter Berry, a man-about-Paris, became her literary adviser and close friend. "Pussy," as Teddy called his wife, fell more and more under the influence of Berry in the immutable course of events. Her novel *The House of Mirth* made her literary reputation, and Walter Berry moved deeper into her life as poor Teddy's senses left him.

Berry was one of the Americans in Paris who had left behind any idea of permanent settlement in a crude United States. He was a New Yorker and a Van Rensselaer, the bluest blood Dutch-America had yet produced. He had been born in Paris and had had a short career as consul to the French and Italian embassies. Being rich, Walter did not have to work. He was a lover of books and gossip who found satisfaction in his own good taste.

It was not until Teddy's third major mental breakdown that Walter became Edith's lover. For all her rational skepticism, she was deeply in love. As for Berry, no one was ever sure. Edith tried for years to talk him into marriage, but he managed to avoid that knot with this determined woman. Walter Berry was a lifetime bachelor. If Edith adored him, he could only shrug and accept her good taste.

Cultured, a lover of the fine things of life, Berry enjoyed friendships with Henry James and Marcel Proust that have been cited as proof of his ability to mingle with the best literary masters. A taster and not a creator of life and art, he was respected by people of talent.

But he was not popular with Edith's friends and admirers, who disliked him with a fury hardly in keeping with their upbringing. Many of Edith's friends claimed that his legally trained, cold, logical mind was a selfish mind, that their relationship was *un amour impossible*. They did not think he was "good enough" for her. His influence on her, outside of literary advice, consisted of belittling her. His views of life were narrow, if rich in detail. His insolent but firm influence on Edith stunted her outlook. Edith let a great deal of his prejudice and bigotry seep into her own thinking, so that some people began to find in her unattractive qualities that she had absorbed from Berry and loyally accepted in dimensions beyond her own reason and experience.

Where Edith saw a wise man of affairs, a complete man of the world, others saw merely a *boulevardier* in high collar, London-cut tailoring, and top hat. Edith was more limber mentally, a writer of moods and emotions who had the ability to touch the mystic rim of life and its fortuity. Berry had no deep philosophical core; he was a shallow superficial creature for all his reading. She might well have been a greater personality, even a better writer, without Berry at her side talking always in his drawling drawing-room voice. It was clear that Berry could not share her insatiable hunger for close understanding with one other human being.

The doubts she must have had affected Edith to the point where her acceptance of his brittle veneer became an act of loyalty. Although it may have been a veneer to her, to Paris it looked like a cold snobbery arising from her arid social position.

Edith was not happy in their relationship, strong as it was on her side, because on his part it was too fluid and flowed away from her. Perhaps, like so many writers, she dreamed of a continual happiness. In her stories there is more than a hint of concern with this difficult business of achieving happiness. And in her fiction are found cultured dilettantes, *boulevardiers,* selfish men about town. She could agree with Baudelaire: "The role of the artist is full self-abnegation."

While she knew what people thought of Walter Berry, she never stopped loving him and never admitted that he would fail her when she needed him. Yet when she was at her most desperate, as Teddy faded from her life, Berry slipped off to Egypt for some embassy post, escaping, some said, his responsibility to Edith.

The picture most people once had of Edith Wharton was of a rather aloof person, almost frigid, at times neurotic, and very much a snob. It was only in 1975 that R. B. Lewis, in his finely researched biography *Edith Wharton,* presented facts to readjust the popular image of her. By presenting certain unpublished documents, he brought to light her overheated, reckless affair with the American journalist Morton Fullerton.

A minister's son, he was a friend of Henry James, and when Fullerton visited America in 1907, he carried out a suggestion from James that he visit Mrs. Wharton. He stayed several days, and it is clear from some notes she made at the time that she, at forty-five, had fallen in love with this man two years younger than herself. When Fullerton returned to Paris, Edith soon followed.

With Teddy out of the way visiting friends, Edith and Fullerton began to see more of each other, lunching, talking, visiting points of interest. From her diaries (which Lewis quotes) it is clear that Edith was being roused to an abnormal, sensual level of passion but was at the same time having doubts. She sensed that this was perhaps her one chance for the release of her imprisoned sexual desires.

As she held back final surrender, Fullerton made it clear that his friendship was of an ardent, direct sexual nature. The affair eventually began with all barriers down, at least on her part. In verse and prose she exalted the physical side of love, like a bright schoolgirl shocked into terrifying sensuality by the drive and power of sex. Even when Teddy came back, the affair, in its first stages, continued for several months at fever pitch. She recorded an urge "to be happy freely, carelessly, extravagantly." She had fully discovered her body. When Edith was a young girl, her mother had kept her ignorant of the realistic physical side of sex and its intimacies. Then her marriage had become sexless very quickly. Now she experienced full sexual release and enjoyed it wildly.

When the first burst of love calmed a bit, she returned to Teddy and to her affection for Walter Berry. Not all her passion for Fullerton was spent, however, and they continued to meet. After World War I they were still friends, meeting often. She wrote to him in 1931 that he was one of two people for whom she felt "total friendship." (Berry was the other.) When Fullerton had problems with other women, Edith tried to help; all through the rest of her life Edith was in contact with Fullerton.

Morton Fullerton had the stuff of a survivor; always in some publisher's or journal's pay, he survived both world wars, living in Paris through the second one. He died in 1952 at the age of eighty-six. His remains rest today in a French cemetery, but not in the one in which Edith Wharton is buried.

The year 1911 was crucial for Edith Wharton's relationship with Teddy. Teddy had not been able to adjust to the new life in the French

city; he had remained an *americain pessimiste*. In September he was
back in the United States taking a cure at Hot Springs, and Edith
sailed for Paris alone. Teddy and Edith had been fighting over houses.
He cried out that she had deprived him of the management of their
house, the Mount, back in Lennox, New York, and also of control of
their money, and had promised that if he were given control, he
would hold on to their home. But even as the ship sailed, Teddy sold
the place. There was little left of his mind.

Humility and forbearance came hard to Edith. She had been
friendly with Henry James since soon after her marriage. Now that
Teddy was sinking into blankness, the marriage destroyed, Edith,
with that determined upper lip often mistaken for snobbery, turned
to James, explaining her dilemma. He tried to console her, for he had
an almost female intuition under his hard shell of dignity and pride.
He knew how Edith was suffering.

Although James was a friendly and portly shoulder in time of
trouble, he did not grasp her remarkable abilities as a novelist. He
thought her writing second-rate. He never saw that her writing was
clearer and crisper than his own involved style and expressed a much
broader knowledge of life and sex, of which James was as innocent as
his walking stick.

By 1912 Teddy was locked away. At the urging of Edith, he had,
under his own free will, entered one of those luxurious private
sanitariums on Lake Constance in Switzerland.

Edith gained a divorce in 1913. Teddy stayed on at Lake Constance
until after World War I, and in 1918 he was taken back to America,
where he died in 1928.

By 1913 Edith Wharton had reached her literary peak with her
novel *The Customs of the Country*. She was also free. With Teddy put
away, there was nothing to face now but Walter Berry and the Great
War. Her mother had died in Paris; she had a brother, Harry, also
living in Paris, but they were not close. There had been another
brother, Fred, who after thirty years of marriage left his wife to run
off with another woman. It was not a particularly romantic elope-
ment, but it did lead to much scandal and a legal mess. Edith sided
with her deserted (and finally divorced) sister-in-law. She and

brother Freddy broke all communication, resulting in one of those dreadful silences and hatreds so common between sisters and brothers in American society, breaks caused chiefly by the scent or loss of money.

Edith, cut off from the family, found in Walter Berry and Morton Fullerton something solid and real. What was left of life she wanted to live fully. As the war approached in August of 1914, Edith was still in Paris, living in a fine modern apartment on the rue de Varenne. She had the eternal English pair: White to butler, Mrs. White to cook. A chauffeur named Cook; a personal maid, Gross; Anna Bahlmann, Edith's ancient governess; and spoiled, yapping little dogs that came snarling and barking at visitors completed her household.

The war caught Edith off base. She had expected to close her flat and spend the fall in England, close to Henry James. But the banks snapped shut, and Edith was left with only two hundred francs on hand. Berry gave her some money, but he too was pressed for cash. Black market exchanges were operating in the open-air *pissotières*. Edith wired London for aid and got back the answer, "Have no money." A cable to her New York bank brought the one word "Impossible." Edith returned to her empty flat. The servants had preceded her to England. She was alone.

She applied for a permit to go to England and then waited as the first days of August burned on the horizon and the gray German war machine tramped in dusty boots toward Paris.

There was sudden unemployment in Paris as the lack of demand for costly gowns, splendid motor cars, and other luxury items threw many out of work. (The great munition factories would later take up this slack.) Edith was asked by her friend the Comtesse d'Haussonville, president of the local French Red Cross, if she would aid in opening "a workshop for the unemployed" to roll bandages.

Edith leaped at the chance. She rented an empty flat, filled it with ninety women, and set them to work making underwear instead of rolling bandages. Winter would soon be there, and, short war or long war, a soldier likes clean underwear. Edith got funds to carry on her workshop by calling on rich Americans still trapped in Paris by lack of transport.

The rest of the war Edith spent organizing French-American relief and writing letters and articles for American publications requesting aid to Europe. In 1916 she received the Cocarde of the Legion of Honor and was honored by Belgium as well.

Then the French Red Cross asked her to report on conditions at the front. Edith was approaching her sixties, but still she went to the front lines, where she peeked at the enemy barbed wire through a spyhole and smelled the dead. Once she was even trapped by a small enemy attack. She would not don pants or boots, so in skirts she tramped through filthy, viscous mud mixed with the carcasses of hundreds of thousands of horses.

At the close of the war she bought an eighteenth-century house and garden just beyond the northern fringe of Paris. Her world was lonely. Henry James was dead, the affair with Fullerton in cold storage. In 1920 Edith Wharton produced *The Age of Innocence,* not a novel of the new age, but a recalling of her own childhood in the 1870s, an exorcism of old ghosts. It earned her the Pulitzer Prize.

After the war Edith represented the permanence of European society in contrast to the instability of the American lost generation. She was pictured as a chain smoker wearing gold-rimmed glasses, a grande dame in her sixties. She sometimes saw Walter Berry, tall and thin in old age, still the dandy with a shock of white hair and a white moustache. Paris thought Berry handsome and wondered what he saw in old Mrs. Wharton, who had lost her trim figure and become what was politely called plump. Even her hair had lost its sheen. She tried the newer fashions and hair styles, but, with that sharp jawline extended by age, the effect was grim.

Berry, for all his high collars and mink-lined overcoats, had ties with the new young Americans in Paris—ties Edith lacked. Harry Crosby, a young cousin of Berry and a nephew of J. P. Morgan, came to Paris with his wife Caresse, and the two became leaders of the wild young set. When Caresse began to act as Berry's hostess, Edith took a great dislike to her, but Caresse only sighed and smiled. "Mrs. Wharton doesn't like me, Uncle Walter."

When Walter Berry had a stroke that left him speechless and

affected both his writing and reading, his personality disintegrated. Edith came to help him. She held Walter's head in her arms; just once he answered her devotion by pressing her hand. After a last stroke killed him on an October day in 1926, Edith went back to the role of the outsider. The Crosbys carried off his ashes and the dead man's fabulous collection of books.

The stock market crash of 1929 merely singed Edith's income. She still had two houses and twenty-two servants. She was suddenly struck by a heart attack in 1937, and, after lingering in a near-coma for two months, she died. Her casket was so large and ornate that it could not be taken down the stairs; it had to be lowered from an upper window. Her wish was to lie as close as she could to the ashes of Walter Berry in the cemetery at Versailles.

Her advice to young writers had been, "All that matters is that you should be free to finish the job." With Willa Cather and Ellen Glasgow, she represented the modern woman novelist, the equal of any American male writer of her period. She wrote from inside the social world of a special class, and she closely observed how women were held back from a full life by the rigid patterns of that class. In a male-dominated world where respectable women were often mere decor, Edith broke out of the mold and let the world know it.

20.
The Age
of Elsie de Wolfe

Mrs. Astor and other women of her day of high social position made houses livable and charming. Knowledgeable about color, texture and fabrics, they gave their homes something new: good taste. It was Elsie de Wolfe who worked for most of them ("I *never* worked; I was offered contracts"), providing them with the confidence to accept a new kind of setting—a less cluttered, more spacious-looking house.

Elsie, like Edith Wharton, was aware of the changing social pattern. In her dry, acid way Edith had written: "The essence of taste is suitability. . . . see how it expresses the mysterious demand of the eye and mind for symmetry, harmony and order." In the book *The Decoration of Homes* (1897) Mrs. Wharton also observed that "a reform in house decoration can originate only with those whose means permit experiments which their taste can suggest. Where the rich demand good architecture [the] neighbors will get it too. . . . "

Records show that Elsie was born in 1875. As a buoyant, unique child growing up in Tuxedo Park, she worked earnestly in amateur theatricals as preparation for a career on the stage, as she later put it, "I did it to support my mother." Under the wing of producer Charles Frohman, she first appeared as a professional actress in 1891 in the play *Thermidor* by Victorean Sarou (the Neil Simon of his time). For the next ten years—in the age of Pierce Arrows and road companies—Elsie toured as an actress. Although she was the star in her last play, *The Wife,* she was well aware of her limitations ("It was clear I was not Sarah Bernhardt") and so decided to leave the stage for good.

In 1900 she went into partnership as a decorator with a friend,

Elizabeth Marbury. They used Washington Irving's old house near Gramercy Park. The partnership lasted ten years.

Such a venture was a risky thing in the early 1900s, for decorating was not an accepted profession then. One unidentified woman in 1905 wrote in a letter, "Decorators? . . . Decaying gentlewomen who have seen better days . . . moving of flower pots and picking out wallpaper for some small sums."

But Elsie was neither decaying nor one who had seen better days. She was pretty and active; she possessed a flaring temper and the ability to convince people that she knew what was good for them. Elsie had no training, as there were no schools for interior decorating, but she had read a magazine article called "Interior Decorating as a Profession for Women." It stated that "a large number of homes belong to the well-to-do members of society who have none of this general cultivation and are well aware of it."

This was grist for Elsie's mill of taste. She had not yet become an original taste-maker; an early photograph shows her reclining in a room of horrors—a decor of overdone cushions with hangings and bric-a-brac cluttering the setting. But she learned fast, her instinct for change leading her on.

Her first large commission, in 1907, was for an exclusive private club which society women had set up to counter the clublife of their husbands. The Colony Club on Madison Avenue above Thirty-first Street had been designed for the ladies by the leading society architect, Stanford White. Anne Morgan, the sister of J. P., liked Elsie's ideas for the interiors, but one of the other committee members questioned the wisdom of giving such an important job to a woman who has had no experience. Stanford White, however, stood by Elsie—"Let the girl alone. She knows more than any of us"—and his fame sanctioned his choice.

Certainly it was a plum for her. While some men of social position were shocked that women would want to club together in this "menace to the American home . . . following the bad habits of their fathers, brothers, husbands, where they smoke and drink," to some the Colony Club was one of the progressive signs that women were moving toward their rights.

Decorator Elsie de Wolfe, prior to her innovative introduction of white-on-white rooms.

Elsie knew this was her big chance to show her potential, and she went all the way. She introduced indoor lattices and the draping of windows and furniture in lots of chintz.

Soon many housewives began to copy the chintz craze on sofas, chairs, doors and windows. It gave a gaiety to interiors of dark fumed oak filled with heavy Victorian furniture, *and* it was not very costly—even the women on Main Street in middle-class flats could afford chintz. Soon every whistlestop town from New York to the West Coast was covered with chintz. It all became a bit too much in time, and the word *chintzy* even today has the connotation of *too much.*

For Elsie it was an ephemeral triumph: "For a while I was known as the Chintz Lady." But by the time that fad faded, a million women were adopting another of her ideas—the invention of the vanity table that offered the convenience of a mirror for making up and for inspecting one's features.

Soon Elsie's firm was receiving more work than it could handle from the fashionable and the socially hopeful, so Elsie could pick her clients with care. She "did" Mrs. William H. Crocker, whose husband was one of the railroad kings who helped seize most of the railroads in the West. The Crocker domain was in Burlington near San Francisco. Next, Elsie worked over the housing of the Ogden Armours of Chicago, banishing the image of a pork packer who was in the money. She dropped down to Minneapolis to handle the decor of the Weyerhausers, who were denuding the forests of the Middle West. Hostesses aching for big-city detail found her work both astringent and exhilarating.

Elsie de Wolfe saw her role as bringing good taste into the average American home. In 1913 she published *The House in Good Taste*. Elsie didn't mince words. She stated: "My business is to preach to you the beauty of suitability. Suitability!" She proudly stated: "I know of nothing more significant than the awakening of men and women throughout our country to the desire to improve their homes."

Elsie made financial progress with "the hard shelled old pirate" Henry C. Frick in the mid-1920s. He had built himself a Medici-style fortress on Seventieth Street and Fifth Avenue. He asked Elsie to advise him about how to furnish the ornate building. She suggested that they go to France to see the famous Wallace collection of rare furniture, which was being offered for sale. Once in Paris, Elsie managed to have the dealer, Jacques Seligman, give them first look at the treasures. Frick was in a hurry, he told Jake (as he called the dealer), but he was ready to buy a fortune in furniture by pointing out what he liked and watching for Elsie's nod of approval. As Elsie later confessed, "My ten percent commission made me a rich woman."

With her clients she continued to insist on expensive and rare items. But to women in the general public she gave basic information: how to get rid of clutter, how to position one's furniture. "To express the personality and character of yourself . . . a woman's environment will speak for her life, whether she likes it or not . . . a house is a dead giveaway . . . accept the standards of other 'imes and adapt them to our uses."

Elsie didn't adhere to her preoccupation with the past for too long. She began to create delicate furniture and to use a great deal of white. In time she turned to white rooms with white furnishings, and to pale settings in pastel tones of off-ivory and pearl gray. Furniture makers began to produce pieces designed along lines consistent with what she insisted was good taste.

Elsie did miss the boat on Art Nouveau; rather, she refused to get aboard. She called Art Nouveau an "avalanche of bad taste . . . those awful chairs, tables supported by flowers . . . mantelpiece of fleurs-de-lis and rushes." Nor did she care for the American decor genius of the moment, Louis Tiffany. She was never to admit she was wrong about Art Nouveau or Tiffany. "Those damn weeds of wood and bronze and *all* curves going around the bend . . . curves, you know, are vulgar; you know that they appeal to the lowest instincts; I mean look at the arses of chorus girls . . . *curves!*"

Elsie did much to destroy a taste for chromes, a cheap, glossy type of color-reproduction that generally featured kittens playing with balls of yarn, shaggy dogs smoking pipes, and sunset in Yosemite. Nor was Elsie much impressed by the hand-colored lithographs of Currier and Ives.

Elsie de Wolfe made middle-class American homelife more cheerful, comfortable and tasteful. In time her ideas seeped down to the level of farm homes and city flats.

And Henry Frick? Did he learn very much from Elsie de Wolfe? His biographer describes him sitting on a Renaissance throne reading the *Saturday Evening Post* while nearby an organist grinds out "Silver Threads Among the Gold." As Elsie once said, "There is often a lot of pig's ear left in those silk purses."

21.
Alice Toklas
and Friend

Eliot Paul, the author of the popular *Life and Death of a Spanish Town* and *The Last Time I Saw Paris,* once remarked, "Just as Boswell made Samuel Johnson, so Alice Toklas built up Gertrude Stein. Without Alice's efforts to get her published, and pushing for all she was worth, Gertrude might just have remained a minor freak of the period."

The truth of this statement is just now coming to light. Only in 1977 did Linda Simon's *The Biography of Alice B. Toklas* bring Alice out of the shadows of anecdotes and gossip, presenting her as a willful, domineering figure, watchful and stern.

A descendant of two brush-merchant families, the Levinskys and the Toklases, Alice was born in San Francisco in April of 1877. The Levinskys were from Exin in Prussia; the Toklases had come from Hamburg. Alice was raised in the turmoil and excitement of a close, rich Jewish family life. Dark and hawknosed, she was not a pretty child. She was, however, an active child, riding bicycles and horses and enjoying art, music and the theater. Bright and alert, she began to search for new horizons at a young age.

In August of 1907, Alice and a girl friend escaped from San Francisco and headed for Paris. In the flat of Sarah Stein, the wife of Michael Stein (Gertrude's brother), Alice met Gertrude, who at one time was sharing a studio with her eccentric older brother Leo (1872–1947).

Alice was to remember that first meeting with her lifelong lover in her old age: "She [Gertrude] was a golden brown presence burned by the Tuscan sun." Alice described her as large and heavy, "with a beautiful modeled unique head." She was pleased to note that she was permitted "to call her Gertrude."

Gertrude Stein was born on February 3, 1875, in Allegheny, Pennsylvania, but she grew up in San Francisco, where the Steins were a well-to-do merchant family. Most of the family money came from an interest in the San Francisco Cable Car Company, and one of Gertrude's brothers, Willy, spent the major part of his adult life on the platform of a cable car, a popular brakeman.

The Steins, like the Jameses, were a traveling family. Along with brothers Willy, Leo and Michael, Gertrude studied languages in Vienna and Paris. Gertrude claimed to be a great reader, but her erudition came mainly from the works of G. Stein. As for music, she admitted that her favorite piece was "The Trail of the Lonesome Pine."

At nineteen Gertrude was at Radcliffe, and she claimed later to have been "the favorite pupil of William James." She did study experiments in automatic writing and was coauthor of a paper entitled "Normal Motor Automatism." She entered Johns Hopkins to study medicine but never received a degree.

Short, dumpy, and solid-featured young Gertrude became aware at an early age that men had no attraction for her emotionally or physically. Her personal feelings were for girls, not boys. She even wrote in an early novel about a lesbian trio on a ship's crossing—a book not published during her lifetime.

In 1903 Leo rented the studio at 27 rue de Fleurus, and Gertrude joined him in September. Sometimes the two dressed alike in brown corduroy outfits and Greek sandals made by Isadora Duncan's brother Raymond, but out of costume the two Steins did not resemble each other. Leo, who was a hypochondriac, full of traumas and neuroses, was tall and thin, with a red-gold beard and a dashing stride. Gertrude had remained short and dumpy; to flatter her, someone once said, "She was like a block of granite."

In the spring of 1903 Leo bought his first Cézanne. The walls of the rue de Fleurus studio eventually held Renoirs, Matisses, Picassos, two Gauguins, Manguins, a nude by Vallotton, a Toulouse-Lautrec, a Daumier, a small Delacroix, and an El Greco (suspect).

The Steins paid five thousand francs (one thousand dollars) for their first Matisse and one hundred fifty francs (thirty dollars) for their first Picasso. Gertrude expected the shine of gratitude in the artist's eyes; she lapped up gratitude. Ambroise Vollard remembered: "Every time I went to an exhibition I saw the Steins, the two brothers [Leo and Michael] and the sister."

Gertrude Stein
in her Paris studio
during the 1920s.

Library of Congress

Gertrude took up Picasso as a cause. Because of her own great yearning for fame, she got Picasso to begin a portrait of her in 1906. There were, she claimed, eighty or ninety sittings, but she did not pose for the final head—Picasso did it from memory. He was working toward his Negro period, inching toward full cubism, and he did a revolutionary picture. The body and hands are in a sort of Renaissance style, dominated by the almost Negro-styled carved head, the face appearing as if ironed free of wrinkles every day. There is no attempt to create a picture of a living person—the eyes do not match in size, and the scale and perspective have been distorted. It is a precubist masterwork of great power, leading directly into Picasso's huge *Les Demoiselles d'Avignon*.

Once Alice and Gertrude became lovers, Alice dominated Gertrude. She cleared a path for her, supervising her friendships, permitting some of them to exist and destroying others. By 1912 Leo was being forced out, although he tried to explain it otherwise: "The presence of Alice was a godsend as it enabled the thing [the affair] to happen without any explosion."

In 1914 Gertrude and Leo parted for good, each going his own way. From then on it was Alice and Gertrude against the world. Brother and sister were never actually to meet and talk again, but they did bow to each other once, when they met by accident on the boulevard Saint-Germain near the Church of Saint-Germain-des-Prés. Leo removed his hat and then politely walked on. Gertrude rushed home to write a story, "How She Bowed to Her Brother." As she put it, "Leo still had his beautiful walk, which was not historic but mythological."

With Alice as maître d', the Stein Saturday nights became a Paris tradition, and the food was good—and free. The talk may have been confusing, but the new painters were on display there, and it was claimed it all helped their sales.

Gertrude wrote, from 1904 to 1906, a book of stories called *Three Lives* which she published herself in 1909. With *Three Lives*, Gertrude boldly announced that she was "the first to write in the twentieth century manner." The book is of interest because it is her first experiment in repeating simple words over and over so that a numbing mood is set up. It is often boring.

Many readers feel that one story in the book, "Melanctha," is the best material Gertrude ever wrote. In a circling, spiraling use of dialect and tempo, it tells a black girl's story. One influence on Gertrude's way-out style was the informal study she made of Baltimore blacks' talk and voice patterns. Another was the fact that she spent most of her life in a foreign environment. As she was to write: "One of the things I have liked all these years is to be surrounded by people who know no English."

Much has already been written about the Paris of Gertrude Stein and Alice B. Toklas. A great deal of the material, recorded with an almost paranoiac ferocity dipped in nostalgia, is actually myth.

The setting of stage and roles has been hindered by the habit of the two protagonists of writing fiction in their autobiographical volumes. Neither Gertrude Stein in *The Autobiography of Alice B. Toklas*

nor Alice in her own texts makes much effort to stick to the facts.
Both Gertrude Stein and Alice were types described by Lord
Byron:

> *One half of the clever people of the world believe they are hated and*
> *persecuted, and the other half imagine they are admired and beloved.*
> *Both are wrong, and both false conclusions are produced by vanity,*
> *though that vanity is the strongest which believes in the hatred and*
> *persecution, as it implies a belief of extraordinary superiority to account*
> *for it.*

Lord Byron also saw clearly the burden the artist must bear: "The
great object of life is sensation—to feel that we exist, even though in
pain. Before fame—or notoriety—overtook them, both Gertrude
and Alice were to know the pain of forcing themselves onto a world
indifferent to them.

Gertrude was mean when crossed; she saw herself as the true
American genius in Paris. And Alice saw to it that all others either
bowed to her or were cast out into darkness. Gertrude could give the
back of her hand rather than the offer of a handshake to a rival.
George Moore, who knew the infighting of artists in Paris, summed
it up perfectly: "A literary movement consists of five or six people
who live in the same town and hate each other cordially."

Paris was the exile base of disillusioned groups of lonely romantics
at a time when Americans went to Paris. Gertrude was quickly
surrounded by sensitive young men from America, many of them
homosexuals who saw in her the Mother of Us All, "the Hebraic
bosom of the Matriarch," as one put it. They defended her, analyzed
her, put her to music, dramatized her works. As her writing became
more obscure and her detractors trampled on her work, she became
a symbol to the select few. Eventually the real person was almost
impossible to see in the clouds of myth-making incense that circled
her life and times. Alice herself was a great myth-maker, never letting
facts confuse her ideas of what the world should see as a vision of
Gertrude.

Gertrude stated, "So Paris was the place that suited those of us

that were to create the twentieth-century art and literature, naturally enough." A remarkable statement from one who was then
known to the general public only by a few nonsensical catch lines: "A
rose is a rose is a rose" or "The pigeons on the grass alas" or, perhaps
her best, in amazing exuberant gaiety, "Toasted Susie is my ice
cream."

Because Gertrude's work did not reach much beyond the American avant-garde of Paris, Alice decided to establish a publishing firm
to print the piled-up Stein manuscripts. Gertrude named the company "Plain Editions." To get the money to print and distribute the
books, they sold one of their Picassos.

The first volume, the 1927 novel *Lucy Church Amiably,* was issued by
Alice in 1931 in an edition of one thousand copies. She noted, "The
event gave Gertrude a childish delight. . . . " This was followed by
How to Write and *Before the Flowers of Friendship Faded.* Although no
great sales resulted, Alice did get the books into the hands of some
bookstores, dealers and reviewers. The name of Gertrude Stein was
becoming known beyond the tight circle of friends and guests at the
rue de Fleurus.

All the time Alice tried to remain in the background. A dark
woman with Indian features and a hint of a moustache, she was the
listener, the adorer, and yet the strong partner in the long friendship
and love affair. People reported that Alice would lay down the law to
Gertrude, and that Gertrude seemed to enjoy being dominated, even
to the point of begging for forgiveness.

Virgil Thomson, who set Stein's *Four Saints in Three Acts* to music,
once stated that Gertrude was in love with Hemingway and would
even have had an affair with him had Hemingway not refused. That
may well be the reason for Alice's dislike of Hemingway.

It was just thirty years after Gertrude's first writings that international fame came to her with *Autobiography of Alice B. Toklas,* her only
successful and most readable book. It is a book of appealing and
wacky charm with a primitive, prattling style. It was her one book
that pleased a vast reading public that didn't give a damn about

avant-garde writing. An American commercial publisher, Harcourt Brace, printed it, the *Atlantic* magazine abridged it, and the Literary Guild took it as a monthly book selection.

There are some who claim that Alice actually wrote *The Autobiography,* or at least contributed a major part of it. "Certainly it is written," Eliot Paul said, "in the style of language Alice spoke at times—an almost bright childish patter with sharp spurs to it and not in many parts related to the truth, for Alice talked for effect, not always for the truth."

Gertrude felt that she was popular with the wrong readers: "When success began, and it was a success, I got lost—completely lost. . . . I was not just I because I became so many people did know me." (Now *that* was a Steinian sentence.)

But in the end she accepted fame—and a trip to America to lecture and to be lionized. Alice saw to the rooms, the fees, and the transportation and steered Gertrude firmly around America.

Gertrude loved the glory, the interviews, the pictures. For her, after so long, *so long,* anticipation had turned into achievement. The book's cover held a circle made up of the words *a rose is a rose is a rose.*

Leo, who came off badly in the book, saw his wit and skill in discovering art usurped by Gertrude as her own. He was outraged. He called the book a "farrago of rather clever anecdotes, stupid brag and general bosh." He pointed out the lies and the wrong dates.

> God, what a liar she is! If I were not something of a psychopathologist I
> should be very mystified. . . . Practically everything she says of our
> activity, our ties before 1911 is false both in fact and implication . . . her
> radical complexes . . . made it necessary practically to eliminate me. . . . I
> simply cannot take Gertrude seriously as a literary phenomenon.

There were others whose lives and views were distorted. The Paris magazine *Transition* issued a booklet, *Testimony Against Gertrude Stein,* in which Matisse, Braque, Tristan Tzara and the Jolases pointed out the mistakes and untruths in *The Autobiography.* Tzara, one of the founders of Dada, called Gertrude and Alice makers of "fraud, [and] egomania." Braque shrugged off her claimed art influence in Paris as nonsense. "Miss Stein understood nothing of what went on around her. But no superegotist does. She never knew French really well, and that was always a barrier. . . . She never went beyond the state of the tourists." Others joined in the act of exorcism.

Alice didn't care what the critical intellectuals said, as Gertrude's fame spread and more Americans came to Paris with hopes of meeting "Lovey" and "Pussy," as they called each other. Alice later published her own story, *What Is Remembered*. The author could have been Gertrude; the style, jokes and japes are the same. Alice and Gertrude, as if by the process of osmosis, sucked up each other's styles and shared absurdities.

Alice, having tasted authorship, then produced *The Alice B. Toklas Cook Book;* in its pages one can find the famous candy recipe in which one of the ingredients is hashish.

With age, Gertrude gave up the cigars she had smoked in imitation of her hero General Grant. The woman who had once been five feet two and nearly as wide grew so thin her bone structure began to show; her head lost its padding and the skull began to push out. Alice cropped her hair short, and she often wore it brushed forward, a lock in the middle of her forehead.

Gertrude died in 1946 after an intestinal operation. Alice, in her written memoir of Gertrude's death, reported, "I sat next to her, and she said to me early in the afternoon, 'What is the answer?' I was silent. 'In that case,' she said, 'what is the question?' "

No other witness reports her last words; was Alice creative here, too?

Life was lonely with Gertrude gone. Money was short; Alice had to sell the Picasso drawings Gertrude had willed her. She became embroiled in a court battle with Gertrude's relatives over the twenty-eight Picasso paintings in the collection left to her in trust, and the collection of cubist works was consigned to a bank vault. Alice Toklas became a Roman Catholic, anxiously asking her priest, "Will this allow me to *see* Gertrude when I die?"

She lived alone her remaining years, bedridden, arthritic, seeing only her maid Yacinta.

Still, Gertrude and Alice were luckier than most of the "lost generation"—they reached old age.

In the end Gertrude's paintings went to the Stein family. But Alice did live long enough to see Gertrude accepted as an important modern author.

On March 7, 1967, Alice, aged eighty-nine, died—twenty-one years after her great love. She is buried in a vault beside Gertrude.

What effect did Alice and Gertrude have on women's lives?

The Stein brothers rather than Gertrude were the true pioneers of their art world. By the time Gertrude wrote of Matisse and Picasso, they were already world famous, and some of their fame rubbed off on her, rather than the other way around. After Leo left Gertrude, she never made a major discovery of an original artist, or even of a fairly good artist.

And serious critics have never accepted Gertrude's own high opinion of herself as an original genius. Even so fond a Stein fan as Mabel Dodge, when writing in praise of Gertrude at the time of the 1913 Armory Show, said: "She has taken the English language and according to many people has misused it, has used it roughly, uncouthly and brutally . . . madly, stupidly and hideously, but by her method she is finding the hidden and inner nature of nature."

But Gertrude and Alice taught the world just how to go about attracting attention. They also stood for being oneself even if that self was unpopular. And their lives were object lessons in the modern woman's search for personal freedom.

22.
The Western Ladies

Before John Steinbeck left California to live in the East, he remarked:

The trouble with any of the real women who helped make the West is that the most interesting of them were so damn disreputable that the social historians skip around them. But for all that, they had a lot to do with making this city, this state, and maybe the whole West fit to live in.

Making the West interesting were, for instance, the escapades of Lily Hitchcock (1842–1929). Lily, the daughter of an eminent army doctor, came to San Francisco at the age of eight in 1851. As her family gradually became socially important, Lily grew into a strikingly handsome girl, what in those days was called a "dashing" girl. She was a firehouse buff, as familiar in the Knickerbocker Fire Company Number Five as the spotted coach dog and the great horses that pulled the steam-fed pumper. She was given to attending fires on the run when she should have been at a ball or some other local social affair. After she was made an honorary member of the Knickerbockers, she even appeared at one ball in her red fireman's shirt and helmet.

She was often seen at cockfights, dressed in men's clothes, shouting for some feathered champion. She played poker with noted gamblers and had a keen eye for an inside draw and a royal flush. Before she was twenty Lily had been engaged to twenty men. She craved emotional stimulus all her life.

Finally there was one man who felt he could marry this ecstatic, irrational fun lover. His name was Howard Coit. When Lily became Mrs. Coit, the bets were down in the city as to how long it would

*Lily Hitchcock Coit
of San Francisco.
She was responsible
for the Coit Tower.*

Author's Collection

last. It didn't last long, as Lily had an incurable taste for change. She went off to Europe to lead a life a little less polite and dull than what Henry James was writing about Americans living abroad. Many regretted to see her leave San Francisco, for they had fond memories of the balls she had given, which featured both the best people and her firemen friends. She would come back from time to time to a suite in the Palace Hotel, surviving into middle age on vitality and the idea that the extreme is a true expression of universal significance.

One day when she was sixty years of age, a shot rang out in her suite, and a man named McClung stepped out, mortally wounded. He had neatly caught a bullet intended for Lily with his chest. He died, and Lily took another trip to Europe. The man who fired the pistol was known to be Alexander Garnett, but no clear explanation of the reason for the shooting was ever given.

Lily returned to San Francisco when she was in her eighties and died in the Palace Hotel in 1929, leaving a fund of $100,000 to build the Coit Observation Tower, which still dominates the city. She also left funds to erect in Columbus Square a statue to the fire laddies of her youth. The statue depicts a group of firemen rescuing a little child. Some think the child's features are modeled after Lily Hitchcock Coit's own.

Among the most prominent personalities in the West were the men who became multimillionaires by building the first railroads to reach the Pacific Coast. Their wives tried to civilize them and to form a proper society, but it was not easy.

One of these men was frugal "Uncle" Mark Hopkins. He didn't drink, didn't smoke, and, having a tender gut, lived off vegetables which he grew and hoed himself in a little garden near his thirty-dollar-a-month cottage. Yet he was worth twenty million dollars. He was lean, long, cautious, and called "the stubbornest man alive"; yet he ran with wild speculators. Hopkins hated waste; he was a string saver, an old-paper hoarder, and he was always picking up bolts, nails and other junk around the railroad shops. He lighted his cottage with a coal-oil lamp and never frittered away his time or his money.

At forty-one Hopkins married his twenty-year-old cousin Mary; they never produced a child. It was she who began to spend their millions on the then bleak Nob Hill, which she saw as a suitable place for mansions and social gatherings.

Mary Hopkins was what used to be called a "constant reader"; she floated on a sea of romantic novels. Totally immersed in their world, she designed herself a castle on Nob Hill, while Uncle Mark chewed his vegetables and said little. Mary had a Palace-of-the-Doges drawing room, a carved English oak dining room (to hold sixty guests), a master bedroom of ebony, ivory and inset jewels, and a library for the reading of poetry, where Browning and Tennyson could be heard by the worthy. Uncle Mark, wispy as an apparition, passed on while asleep in a train and was interred in a rose marble mausoleum that cost $150,000.

Mary became "America's Richest Widow," and she liked the title.

She was fifty and still reading novels when she began building houses all over the country. A château at East Barrington modeled on Chambord cost her two million. San Francisco's society boggled its eyes at it, but Mary Hopkins didn't flinch. She was imperious and dictatorial, and the town enjoyed her eccentricities, such as entertaining wild artistic guests and worshipping furniture like a fanatic.

One day a young man called on Mary and asked to see her furniture. He was Edward T. Searles, twenty-eight, an interior decorator by profession. The two hit it off at once and spent the day touching chairs and fingering draperies. Mary Hopkins and Searles shared three pleasant years of courting furniture, eyeing cabinets, and unrolling rugs. Then, in a true love match, they were married in 1882.

After nearly ten years of contented marriage among Louis XII chairs, Mary Hopkins Searles died, leaving her vast railroad fortune to Edward Searles.

An adopted son of Mark Hopkins at once took the will to court. The case was settled out of court for between eight and ten million dollars, and Edward T. Searles retired to live in peace among the Chippendales. As for the Hopkins mansion, in time it was torn down, and the Mark Hopkins Hotel, known as the Top of the Mark, arose in its place.

Mrs. Leland Stanford was the wife of the railroad king who became governor of California. Because of her husband's passion for horses, she lived on a stud farm with 2 racetracks, 60 acres of trotting park, 150 hired hands, 60 stallions always at stud or ready for it, 250 brood mares, and 250 colts and fillies, for whom 60 acres of carrots were grown. (Stanford's interest in horses resulted in his hiring a camera expert named Eadweard Muybridge to try to discover if a horse kept all its feet off the ground at any certain time in its running pace. With a series of cameras set off by trip cords, Muybridge proved that at a certain instant it did, and in doing so he practically invented the motion picture.)

Women like Mrs. Stanford, although of domineering, driving mien, sometimes fade into the background when the history of their

Mrs. Leland Stanford,
whose belief in spiritualism
led to the founding
of Stanford University.

California Historical Society

times is written, because often the men take on larger stature and become myths. Mrs. Stanford, however, gave the family its real place in the West. She was known as a woman with a genuine interest in the arts, music and the newest literary trends. Her art knowledge, based on the good taste of the times, drew her to Pre-Raphaelite painters such as Millais, Rossetti, Hunt and Burne-Jones. And while concerts and operas in San Francisco were simply social events to most of the city's wealthy people, Mrs. Stanford entertained the visiting musical figures and talked to them sensibly of their work. She also had a keen interest in and desire to investigate the unknown.

But these interests were suddenly overshadowed by a long-awaited event: the birth of a child. The Stanfords had seemed to be barren until, after twenty years of marriage, they produced Leland, Jr., in 1868. He was at once marked by his mother and father for education in the arts, music and languages—the family traveled in order to give the child an ardent and idyllic interest in the better

things. He had already become an expert wood carver when wry
destiny, unimpressed by rich hopes, killed the boy at sixteen by
typhoid in Florence, Italy.

It was a cruel blow, and perhaps it unsettled Mrs. Stanford's touch
with reality, for she turned to table-rapping as a means of reaching
the dead. Maude Lord Drake, a spiritualist who claimed divine
origin, suggested to Mrs. Stanford that the Stanfords found a college
as a memorial to their dead son (Maude Lord Drake was later
exposed as a fraud during a table-rapping session), and so Stanford
University opened in October of 1891. Today all three Stanfords lie
buried together on the campus, as if keeping watch on the doings of
students and officials.

23.
Hetty Green's Fortunes

Bernard M. Baruch was once asked who, in his opinion, had the greatest understanding of money, high finance, and the workings of Wall Street. He said, "J. P. Morgan and Hetty Green, and I'd hate to be asked who was the better at the game of successfully manipulating money on a very grand scale."

Hetty Green was born a Robinson in New Bedford in November of 1835, an heiress to two family fortunes made in the whaling industry. For all her wealth, she had a stern upbringing. She reported later in life, "My father told me never to give anyone anything, not even a kindness . . . " She added, "I am not a self-made woman. I was born rich." But the family fortune, large as it was, was peanuts compared to the $150 million or more that Hetty piled up through her knowledge of and cunning in the money markets and her keen understanding of the gyrations and genuflections of Wall Street.

Hetty is remembered today as being shabby, stingy and eccentric. Yet in her youth she had personal charm and grace, although she was a rebel and had a sharp tongue. She dressed well and went to good schools. At fifteen she went to a Boston finishing school, where she read through the Bible three times. Hetty was a handsome girl, and her father took care to instill in her the idea that most men were fortune hunters.

From the many family battles over wills and inheritances (this seemed to be the family's way of life), Hetty early learned the power of money and the skills required to get it and hold on to it. Sent to New York with money to buy a new wardrobe, she invested the money instead and showed a good profit.

At that time Hetty was active socially, and when the Prince of Wales, who was traveling as Baron Renfrew, came to New York, she danced twice with him. Hetty had been introduced to him by someone with wit as "The Princess of Whales."

The Civil War destroyed the whaling industry by taking its ships for war service and giving rise to rebel raiders, so Hetty and her father moved to New York City permanently. She was young, but already had a high-keyed articulate manner. On her father's advice she began to show interest in men who were already rich; they could not be fortune hunters. Her father introduced Henry Green to her. He was an older man, rich, handsome, and a world traveler. Born in Vermont, he had become wealthy trading in tea, silk, hemp and tobacco in the Philippines. Hetty thought that he spent too much money on gifts and on his tailoring, but he could speak Chinese, and certainly his was a character different from that of the usual available young man.

Her father died before the romance flowered fully, leaving Hetty a million dollars. When an aunt died leaving a rather confused will, Hetty produced a will that made her the major heiress. The will was called a forgery, and a notorious series of hearings, court cases and trials followed. Millions of words were produced as testimony, relatives fought relatives, and all fought Hetty. Handwriting experts testified against her, but Hetty claimed her aunt had asked her to write the appendage to the will.

Henry Green was a witness in her favor, and after the lengthy days in court they were married in July of 1867. She was thirty-three; Henry Green was forty-six. He signed a document stating that his wife would not be liable for his debts and that he would furnish her support. She felt that the ten-dollar gold coin her new husband paid the minister after the wedding was a bit too much.

They sailed to England to honeymoon and stayed there; some said she still feared being charged with forgery. Henry Green didn't seem to mind Hetty's eccentricities, even her occasional diet of raw eggs and crackers. Hetty didn't approve of his habits of drinking rum and smoking cigars, but she was in love and not yet so unyielding as she later became. In England, the Greens were in the social swim. She was presented to Queen Victoria, and she and Henry attended balls and were weekend guests in the best castles. They lived well in a flat in the Langham Hotel.

Henry Green was a director of several London banks, and Hetty began dealing in government bonds and buying gold. She did well, making nearly two million dollars in one year. In just one day she managed to collect $200,000. She was respected as a rich American moving among the best people, and if they found her a bit bizarre, well, "she was, after all, an American."

In 1868 she gave birth to a son, Edward Robinson Green, usually called Ned. In 1871 there was a daughter, Hetty Sylvia Green. Hetty was a good mother. Her only prominent sign of eccentricity at this time was her dislike of spending money on her clothes. She began to look a bit shabby, and laundered only the hems and the ruffles on the bottoms of her petticoats.

The fashionable life abroad began to bore her in time, and the family moved back to the United States in 1875. They went to live with Henry Green's mother in Bellow Falls, Vermont. In this placid environment Hetty dressed even more shabbily and did not bathe very often. In time she became actually grimy.

Yet Hetty was one of the most brilliant women in the matters of high finance that America ever produced. Her wisdom in banking and real estate was remarkable: she was able to best most of the big brokers of Wall Street. She made fortunes during national panics and depressions and could foreclose on a railroad or a block of buildings "quicker than you could say Jack Robinson." Henry Clews, an authority on money, called Hetty "one among a million of her sex."

She loved her children, but when Ned, at fourteen, injured his knee, she treated it first at home; then, in shabby dress, she took him to a free clinic in New York as a charity patient. The ruse was discovered, and because of her neglect the boy lost his leg. It was removed by a noted surgeon, who sent her a bill for $5,000, an outrageous fee for the time. Hetty refused to pay it. Henry Green separated from his wife, sold the remains of his stock holdings, and paid the surgeon's bill.

It was not just Henry's dislike of Hetty's ways that separated

Hetty Green on Wall Street.

them. Hetty could never condone failure, and Henry had invested heavily and lost most of his fortune; he owed the broker J. J. Cosco nearly $14 million.

J. J. Cosco and Company seized over half a million dollars of Hetty's money as partial payment for her husband's debts. She was outraged, but settled for a recovery of over $400,000 and then moved her securities of $25 million from J. J. Cosco to the Chemical National Bank, using boxes carried in a hired wagon.

Many people hardly knew she had a living husband, but in fact it was not a mean separation. Actually, Hetty often met Henry in the street outside his club to talk over family matters. The pair remained friendly, and when Henry was dying Hetty took him into her dismal room in Hoboken and nursed him tenderly. Whatever else Hetty had, she also had her softer moments and a deep family interest which she hid from the public, who knew her only as the nation's greatest woman financier, dealing in stocks, gold, railroads, ranches, real estate, theaters—wherever her keen mind could see a chance for a good profit.

Hetty often needed legal help because of law suits, but she hated lawyers for what she considered their dishonorable and unethical ways of stripping the bones of their clients. She felt that justice was a mockery, that lawyers fed like jackals on court cases, and that judges could be bought. She often dismissed her lawyers, usually without paying their fees. She carried a pistol, she said, "Not in fear of thieves, but for lawyers." She found accountings by courts and lawyers' fees outrageous and went to court to fight them. She quoted Shakespeare, "Let us begin by killing all lawyers." She did poke lawyers hard with her umbrella, a deadly weapon in her hands, and once threatened an unfriendly lawyer with the heel of her shoe, ready "to paste him in the face." When lawyers attacked her in court, she would often flop to her knees, lock her hands in a gesture of prayer, and call on the Lord for help against these legal sharks.

The umbrella, a molting seal cape, and a bit of hat on her graying hair became Hetty's trademarks. She was no recluse—Hetty liked attention and gave many press interviews. At the Chemical National Bank, where she was given a free office as a favored client, she enjoyed sitting on the floor cross-legged, working with the boxes that contained her stocks and bonds, mortgages, and records. She never took advice. She would seek out a stock or a bit of land that seemed promising, buy it, and surprise many so-called experts by making a fortune. She expanded into hotels, ranches, even two cemeteries; she held mortgages on nearly thirty churches.

As she explained her success, "There is no great secret in making a fortune. I believe in getting in at the bottom and out at the top. All you have to do is buy cheap and sell dear."

Hetty had the cash for good deals that would suddenly show up. Sensing that the panic of 1905 was coming, she turned many of her holdings into cash and soon was making fortunes lending money to those caught short. She usually had $30 million cash on hand for quick loans, and she would carry on her person $200,000 in negotiable bonds.

Hetty liked the feel of the physical symbols of her wealth: the bonds, the stocks, the contracts. She had dozens of safe deposit boxes in various cities across the nation and carried their keys on a chain around her waist. Meanwhile, her wealth benefited the nation by building railroads, hotels, churches and ranches.

Personally she continued to live in cheap rented rooms in Hoboken, paying a rent of fourteen dollars a month including lights and heat under the name of C. Dewey. C. Dewey, better known as Cutie Dewey, was her pet Skye Terrier.

She ate second-rate food, buying it in bulk. Hetty believed in eating onions for health and carried them around to chew on, a practice which didn't add to her very few charms. But she remained healthy and sturdy, and put in a ten- to twelve-hour workday on her various projects. The only known splurging she ever did was to buy her son Ned $100 worth of firecrackers every Fourth of July. The boy was her messenger; she loved him and his sister, even if she did keep them on short rations and dress them in frowsy clothing.

When Ned was still a boy, Hetty educated him in her own philosophy. Hetty gave him some rules, none of which she followed herself: "Never speculate on Wall Street; never maintain an office; eat slowly; don't stay up all night; don't drink ice water; and keep out of drafts." As Ned grew older, Hetty gave him more and more responsibility with large sums of money.

Like his mother, he was a good businessperson who handled his fortune shrewdly. Ned grew to be six feet four inches tall and to weigh 300 pounds. In spite of his mother's teachings, he became a sportsman, a playboy and a notorious hedonist. Stumping about on his wooden leg, he kept a yacht, a stamp collection, rare coins, and a mistress, the red-haired Mabel Harlow, whom he didn't dare marry while his mother was alive. He drove one of the first autos, had a private railroad car, smoked cigarettes, and ran for the governorship of Texas as a Republican.

Sylvia, Hetty's daughter, led a dismal life as a child and even later was always under her mother's frugal control. In 1909, at age thirty-eight, she married Matthew Astor Wilks, who was twenty-five years her senior. Hetty had herself done up for the wedding with beauty treatments, and she even wore a striped silk dress of opalescent tints looped with lace medallions.

Hetty's major problem was avoiding tax collectors. Three states claimed she owed them taxes, and by 1913 there was a federal income tax. For years Hetty changed addresses and names frequently and refused to give her address in order to avoid tax collectors—not paying taxes was a game she enjoyed.

But by 1910 her dog Dewey was dead, and she had become aware that she too was mortal, for her own health was failing. In 1916 she had her first stroke. Another stroke followed, but she still watched the stock ticker and continued to buy and sell. She never grew foolish or feeble-minded, even in her last days.

Hetty Green made no fuss about dying. "I do not know what the next world is like. But I do know that a kindly light is leading me and I shall be happy after I leave here." She died on July 3, 1916, at the age of eighty-one. She was buried at Henry Green's side in Bellow Falls. Hetty left nearly everything—in trust—to her son and daughter, with instructions that each was to get only the income from $60 million until Ned was fifty-eight and Sylvia fifty-five.

Hetty Green was a remarkable woman, one of the greatest manipulators of money, land holdings and stocks the nation had yet produced. The New York *Sun* stated, "Hetty Green . . . contributed to the development of the country, a service not to be held in contempt."

Hetty had explained her existence simply: "I am in earnest, go my own way. I take no partners, risk nobody else's fortune, therefore [to Wall Street] I am Madame Ishmael, set against every man."

24.
Jackie Yes,
Jackie No

It is almost impossible to pick the Queen Bees of today with any degree of accuracy. Tastes, fashions, philosophies change, so one can only guess. Most likely Eleanor Roosevelt will be one; perhaps one or two other women will be accepted as taste-makers and mode-setters of the 1960s and 1970s.

Jacqueline Kennedy Onassis must be included. Certainly she turned the rather fusty White House into a place of great charm, with antique furnishings throughout its rooms and masterworks of American artists of all periods on its walls. She sent into storage much of the formal china and gave to White House gatherings gracefulness and uniqueness—a shine that was lacking in the regimes before hers.

True, the Kennedy years are no longer looked upon as Camelot, a knightly era of splendid social charm, wit and manners. Tragic contradictions have arisen. But there was a kind of magic in those years when Jacqueline was the First Lady. With her quiet voice, its little-girl quality out of key with her appearance, Jackie moved among well-dressed intellectuals, a figure of fashion and grace, providing encouragement for many artists. Later exposure has shown that some of the magic was pure image, but then the function of magic is to set up sublime mystery and allure.

In the world of style Jackie blazed trails by the way she cut her hair and the way she wore her clothes. Several Washington hostesses have said that it wasn't the real Jackie but the splendid image of Jackie that "made so many women dress better, made a lot of dowdy

wives from the corn belt go to superior hairdressers and get themselves into more stylish fashions." One observer commented:

> Jackie, during the Kennedy years, gave Washington's social scene a face
> lift. Maybe she was greedy, extravagant, publicity-mad, maybe she did
> do cruel things to others by her autocratic manner, as some have said.
> Well, it only proves she was human and vulnerable. I think her critics
> forget that—she was so damn vulnerable.

History has not returned the final verdict on her yet. But as an
image she cannot be ignored. She was always news, presenting a
façade of imperturbability. The mirage of the uplifting Kennedy
years (and it was mostly a myth) could not have existed if most
people hadn't wanted it. The makers of fairy tales—Hans Christian
Andersen, the Grimm Brothers, Walt Disney, the creator of Oz—
gratify a secret desire in most of us. Jacqueline Kennedy Onassis was
nominated for and accepted as a fairy princess by public acclaim.

Her direction in life was bred into her from birth. She was born
Jacqueline Lee Bouvier in 1929. Her father, a sporting gentleman and
a stockbroker on Wall Street, was the famous (or notorious) "Handsome Jack" or "Blackjack," John Bouvier. Her mother was a New
York socialite, born into a dynasty of bankers and real estate kings.
Jackie was presented to the world at Southampton, Long Island,
during the era of the "best people," and she was raised by a solidly
Republican and firmly Roman Catholic family. The Catholics of
Long Island, New York City, Boston, Philadelphia—rich and socially
ambitious—were making their bid for entry into high society, and
the Buckleys, the Kennedys, the Dohenys, the McDonnells, the
Kellys (who produced Princess Grace), and the Bouviers were
prominent among them.

Jackie differed from the first generation of monied Catholics; at
her debut a society reporter wrote, "Her classic features . . . poise . . .
her background is strictly old guard." It was this old-guard background that the climbing Kennedys were seeking, having come up
through ward politics. With strange speculations and odd deals,

Joseph Kennedy set his brood to hunting for high position. Jackie was the product of fine private schools, some years at Vassar, and a period in Paris spent taking pictures for the *Times-Herald,* during which time she covered the coronation of Queen Elizabeth II.

The Camelot myth begins with two versions of how Jackie met John F. Kennedy: either she asked for a press interview or they were seated across from each other at a dinner party. In any case, John Kennedy was smitten, and they were married in September of 1953. Archbishop Cushing of Boston performed the wedding ceremony. Arthur had taken Guinevere as his bride. And, as in the tales of the knights of the Round Table, beneath the surface of honor and chivalry lurked strange things—the irritants of power, the frailties of faithfulness promised.

Jackie had a gift for decorating and loved doing over whole houses. In fact, John complained that there never was a fully livable set of rooms. Jackie dedicated herself to doing over the White House. Here, she felt, was the biggest challenge she had ever faced. Under her direction, painters, carpenters and rug layers did over room after room, sparing only Lincoln's bed and some of Teddy Roosevelt's game heads.

The decline of Camelot was not her fault. Wrote French Ambassador Herve Alphand of John F. Kennedy in April 1962, "His desires are difficult to satisfy without raising fears of scandal and its use by his political adversaries." Alphand, the envoy to Washington from 1956 to 1965 and a personal friend of the Kennedy family, added that "such a fall will come perhaps one day, for he does not take sufficient precautions in this puritan country." Ambassador Alphand spoke highly of Jacqueline Kennedy and of her efforts to redo the White House and to improve its cuisine with a French chef.

Jackie *was* extravagant. She had a naked, unsublimated drive to spend. Both her husbands lost their tempers over the cost of her wardrobes. In 1961 she spent over $150,000 on clothes; in 1962 she raised the ante to over $160,000 just for gowns, mostly by Cassini, Dior and Balenciaga. Her hairdresser was paid over $40,000 during one year. But, aided by these assets, she did become a style-setter.

Was Jackie as simple, as indifferent to the interest in her life and to the ways of the world, as she seemed? People close to her do not think so. Historian Arthur M. Schlesinger, a keen observer, recognized in her an awareness and an "all-seeing and ruthless judgment." Several people who knew her said almost the same thing about the private Jackie. Schlesinger sums her up this way: "Her response to life was aesthetic, rather than intellectual or moralistic."

Given her upbringing and habits, it seemed strange she could become interested in so uncouth a self-made rough diamond as Aristotle Onassis. She and John had been guests on his fabulous yacht, and after the death of the President, Jackie was often a visitor on board. It would seem both she and Onassis had compulsive drives and ideas that brought them together. Perhaps Onassis felt that with her as his wife he would rise in the world's estimation, at least among the jet setters, or that marrying the beautiful widow of an American President might enhance his business projects. As for Jackie, there are many hypotheses, even that she loved the man, but certainly his ability to pay for her wild shopping sprees and her demands for more and more luxury could have been a factor. She was nearing forty, he was sixty-eight; both desired to flaunt their grandeur and attract attention. The marriage appears to have been a failure, and two published books on Onassis's life frankly state that he was preparing to divorce Jackie just before he died.

To be a Queen Bee, a woman does not have to be perfect or noble or even highly intellectual; she must, however, attract others and offer something—often vital rather than valid—to her world. And that Jackie did by skillfully playing out a legend and thus influencing modes and style for a generation of American women.

She had often been heard to say, "Will I never have privacy?"

A Washington friend of hers commented, "If one stands in the sun, one does cast shadows, doesn't one?"

25.
The Baez Touch

Joan Baez demonstrates the Greek philosopher Plato's statement, made over two thousand years ago, that music has a revolutionary power. "Forms and rhythms in music are never changed without producing changes in the most important political forms and ways. A new musical style goes on to attack laws and constitutions, displaying the utmost impudence." Ms. Baez is a perfect example of Plato's law.

Joan Baez has been the leader in the rise of American folk music with a timely acid bite. Her audiences included both the avant-garde and the ordinary citizen. Her folk music, the critics have said, is drama accessible, and the mood is easy. No one listens to her passively.

Still in her thirties, Joan Baez is part of the history of the form. An unknown back in 1959, she was a success at the Newport Jazz Festival, a new face among such stars as Earl Scruggs, Jean Richie and Odetta. With the first notes, Joan's clear soprano voice made it evident that here was a new star. Robert Shelton of the *New York Times* wrote that her singing was "as lustrous and rich as gold, unwinding like a spool of satin."

Born in 1941, Joan from the start led the life of a drifter. At an early age she knew the many sides of New York City, Boston and Palo Alto. Not that she was underprivileged—she often traveled with her father, a physicist with UNESCO and a former Harvard professor, when he attended intergroup conferences.

In 1959 Joan was in the Fine Arts school of Boston University, and she used to go out to sing in cafés and small clubs around Boston. With her rich voice she became a local favorite in a short time; she also developed a fundamental skepticism concerning political events. The combination of her compelling style and the earnestness of her effort to make of folk music a protest stronger than the usual lament turned her music into a critical and powerful tool. As she became famous, she began to appear for UNESCO and CORE.

She usually appears on stage without any dramatic pose; in fact, some see in her an Indian kind of dignity. On stage she attacks the arpeggio chords on her guitar and simply begins to sing. In a seemingly effortless fashion, she projects a world in need of love and understanding. She doesn't milk the audience for applause, but leaves the stage as calmly as she came on. She has been called "genuine, unassuming."

Joan claims she has no one-track approach to folk music. She does not specialize or study the learned speculation of folk musicologists. When she hears a new song that touches her, she likes to try it. She picks from what is there; and, while her interpretation is her own, she never mauls or destroys the original by overlaying it with a fancy style.

During the protest years of the sixties and the early seventies, when it was dangerous to protest openly because the FBI and the police were using clubs and mace to keep the anti–Vietnam War activists from spreading their ideas among the young on the streets and on the campus, Joan was active around Berkeley. Married and a mother by this time, Joan still showed a fearless indifference to public opinion. She was eventually jailed for her attitudes toward the war and the unholy pressures of the Nixon attitudes toward youth in protest. She admitted to being a free woman, a battler for women's rights. She also admitted, almost casually, that she had at one time been in love with another woman.

Unlike Elvis Presley, who did so much to bring on the new revolution of folk sound, Joan does not dress oddly, prance about a stage, or try to develop a personality that is freaky and way out in order to introduce a new metaphor for music. She simply presents herself as a voice and a sound. And somehow, one senses that she is also presenting truth, beauty, honesty and love.

How right Plato was to think of certain music, and certain music makers, as producing "important political changes, attacking laws . . . displaying the utmost impudence." It is to Joan Baez's credit that her impudence—on the college campuses, in the tear-gassed streets, and in the outrage against the horrors of a dreadful war—demonstrated that impudence could have dignity without losing its power or its validity. Numerous recordings of her image and her music will preserve, for the future, the look and sound of a modern woman in the foreground of direct protest against the wrongs of her time.

26.
Ladies of the Press

The play *The Front Page* never mentions a woman reporter or editor. Yet the authors Ben Hecht and Charles MacArthur knew better. Alicia Patterson, one of Harry Guggenheim's several wives, established one of the most interesting newspapers in America, the Long Island *Newsday*. By modernizing its format and seeking out new kinds of stories, her paper influenced the renovation of a major portion of the American press.

Women, in fact, have managed to publish some of the most interesting newspapers in the nation. Cissy Eleanor Medill Patterson (1884–1948), the first woman publisher of a major city newspaper, made a splash with the Washington *Times-Herald*. A mercurial type, she brought zip into the running of a newspaper. And as owner of a private railroad car, *The Ranger,* she was one of the few women who dared to prove that such cars were not only for male tycoons. She had seven sets of slipcovers for the seats in the car, one for each day of the week. And she alerted florists along the way of her travels to stand by with loads of fresh flowers.

Today many think that the best newspaper in Washington is the *Washington Post,* which broke open Watergate. The publisher, Katharine Graham, became one of the heroines of the American journalism when her paper uncovered the greatest criminal misdeeds ever perpetrated directly from the White House. She showed great courage in standing by her editors and reporters when it looked as if both she and the paper would face huge libel suits if the crimes of the Nixon gang could not be proven.

These women publishers proved that they did not need male caricatures of editors out of the play *The Front Page* to run an intelligent newspaper in an age when the styles of Hearst, Pulitzer and Colonel McCormick had long been out of step with the multifaceted, multifragmented world. By studying one of them in detail, one can point up the problems still facing women in the craft (perhaps an art?) of running a big-city daily newspaper.

Dorothy Schiff was publisher of the *New York Post* until 1977. While the *New York Post* may not have been one of the great journals, it was a gallant survivor in a town that killed off large newspapers. New York had seen the departure of the *Sun,* the two *World*s, the *Herald-Tribune,* two Hearst papers, the *Telegram* and others, leaving New York City, which once boasted of two dozen dailies in several languages, with the *New York Times,* the *Daily News,* and the *New York Post.* "Survival is all" was both Dorothy Schiff's and the *Post*'s motto. As a paper the *Post* tried to be intelligent and lively while maintaining a high standard of integrity.

The *Post* had been founded by Alexander Hamilton. ("Naturally I would have been on Jefferson's side," said Dorothy Schiff.) After many changes and periods of inertia, it became J. David Stern's in the 1930s. Stern revitalized the paper, making its policy liberal. It was one of the handful of newspapers in the nation to support Franklin Roosevelt and the New Deal.

Dorothy Schiff, a relative of Stern, took over as publisher in 1939. When the *Post* became a monopoly afternoon newspaper, Dorothy began to show her merits—and, according to some, her faults. But she ran a tight ship. Everyone knew she was the boss. She was a penny watcher for the thirty years she kept the *Post* afloat, even as some thought it was moving in a slow cadence toward death.

Since the takeover of Rupert Murdock, the devouring English press lord, some of Dorothy's old staff members have called her patronizing, castrating, imperious, elegant, bitchy; others, however, have suggested that she was timid, kind, generous and sad.

In any case, during her reign Dottie Schiff showed much courage. She destroyed the nasty power of Walter Winchell in a series of reputation-shattering articles—a dangerous task, since Winchell saw himself as untouchably powerful both as a social gossip and as a political force. She was not afraid to face the fury and rage of Lyndon Johnson when he cursed the *Post* for columns attacking his vanity and his greed for power. And before it was fashionable to lament the conditions of blacks and Puerto Ricans, Dorothy was condemning the way they were treated.

She had idiosyncrasies, but she held to her priorities. Her exposure of the secret Nixon slush fund in 1952 led to the famous Checkers Speech. Back when few papers dared attack Joe McCarthy and his raucous staff, long before kicking at Joe McCarthy became a popular game, the *Post* raised its voice against the gutter methods of the senator from Wisconsin. Dottie studied the House Un-American Activities Committee and its crucifying of the suspected and innocent, and it too got its lumps from the *Post*. She also held back scurrilous columns about Jackie Onassis, deeming them unfair and in bad taste.

Because the *Post* had to economize—it lacked the coffers of the *Times* or Scripps-Howard—Dorothy developed her own bright people. Jules Feiffer, Nora Ephron, Jimmy Breslin and many others worked at the *Post*. One *Post* reporter remarked that "She was like Churchill when she began a conversation. You felt it was worth listening to and you didn't dare interrupt."

The future of the *New York Post* in new hands is not clear. But in three decades this remarkable woman publisher showed great courage and staying power beyond that of many publishers.

Dorothy Schiff may well be among the last independent newspaper publishers of a big-city paper. More and more, it is becoming the norm for every large American city to have one major monolithic newspaper owned by a newspaper chain.

One newspaper that is dominating an area and era is the *Los Angeles Times,* which has the morning field to itself in Southern California. For the past twenty years a woman was one of the powerful forces swaying the paper's policy and giving a personal color to the publication. Dorothy Buffum Chandler hovered over the *Times* with the gaze of a mesmerist.

She began its "Women of the Year" awards, in which a dozen or so local women were honored annually. That the majority were of small importance didn't matter—to be "one of Buffy's women" was a valued social accolade. Only when age recently led her to retire from the paper was "Women of the Year" laid to rest by the editorial department.

Buffy determined the cultural pattern of the city of Los Angeles. She served as a regent on the Board of the University of California and dominated the music and arts organizations. The Music Center, the city's offering to culture and drama, was Buffy's great creation. Her reward is the *Dorothy Chandler Pavilion* in the Music Center, one of the few monuments named, and deservingly so, for a living person.

27.
The Time
of Le Gallienne
and De Mille

Eva Le Gallienne, born in London in 1899, combined her individual desire to express herself as an artist with her urge to serve the public by founding an organization that for over forty years has brought avant-garde theater and works of such classic masters as Shakespeare, Ibsen and Shaw to an audience of limited income. She was aware of the existence of an intelligent public who were overlooked because their artistic tastes did not match their incomes. Eva's monument was her Civic Repertory Theatre on unfashionable Fourteenth Street in New York City. It represented one of the boldest, most adventurous advancements that had yet been made in American culture.

It is the irony of history that fame has a way of bouncing about, and no one knows for sure on whom it will finally come to rest. Eva's father was a once-famous Victorian-Edwardian poet, a romantic, footloose, flamboyant figure in the style of Shelley and Keats. As for Eva, few saw her as more than "that girl of Richard's." Yet today the poet is hardly remembered or read, while Eva is well known. Eva, however, has remained faithful to his memory. In her book *With a Quiet Heart,* she wrote; "I suppose it's natural to be proud of one's parents and I am proud of mine." His daughter said she saw him as "a mercurial being . . . a patient worker, an understanding friend." She added, "Brilliant, cruel . . . dangerous."

Eva grew up in England and in France, an international child of a failed marriage. She came early to the idea that the world was a stage, and so an actress she would be.

By 1926, when she started the Civic Repertory Theatre, she was already a successful actress, having starred in *Liliom* and *The Swan.* In a

Eva Le Gallienne as Marguerite Gautier, "The Lady of the Camellias."

neighborhood that was nearly a slum, she found a decaying theater
set down between an ancient armory and some sweatshops. All the
buildings shook whenever the Sixth Avenue El trains passed. The
theater, built in 1866, had come down to being a burlesque house;
that failing, it had then been rented to fly-by-night Italian players.
After that it was a home for mice and spiders. Eva, with the aid of
meager private patronage, brought in plasterers and painters, and up
went the electric sign CIVIC REPERTORY THEATRE. The Fourteenth
Street Association, delighted to find a tenant, put up a street banner:
WELCOME LE GALLIENNE.

Few uptown had much hope in the foolish project. But boldly Eva
posted the names of some of the plays that were to be offered:
Chekhov's *Three Sisters* (the Russian writer was not then fully ac-

cepted as a master dramatist on these shores) and Shakespeare's *Twelfth Night,* along with Ibsen's serious dramas *The Master Builder* and *John Gabriel Borkman.* As she puts it, "It was an attempt to provide the people . . . with a popular priced classic repertory theatre."

Success came, even though economic constraints pressed. Over the years, with the help of extra funds and support, the theater presented great plays and served as a show place for fine actors and as a training platform for young hopefuls. And over it all Eva presided as producer and actress.

Eva had the ability both to survive and to attract attention. She liked to tell how, as a small child in Paris, she would put her straw hat on the ground in the *carrefours* of the Bois and boldly sing out a collection of folk songs in French, Dutch, English and German. She would sing nursery songs and also the bawdy music hall hits. Crowds would collect, and little Eva, aged eight, would pass the hat. It was this same awareness of the connection between art and the purse that enabled her to keep her theater alive and active during the hard years. Her education for it? At fifteen she had finished her educaton at the College Sevigne; from then on her life was the stage.

In the early 1930s Eva took her theater on tour with such plays as *Romeo and Juliet,* three works by Ibsen, and a marvelous version of *Alice in Wonderland.* Eleanor Roosevelt came to see the *Alice,* and Eva, in her costume as the White Queen, greeted the President's wife from the stage.

Eva was invited to the White House for tea, and there FDR's people promised to set up a fund to establish a national theater through Eva Le Gallienne. As chief assistant to FDR, Harry Hopkins made a solemn promise to send her an official confirmation of federal subsidies of as much as $100,000 for her theater. She remembered, "That was the last I ever heard of the subject." Harry Hopkins never answered any of the letters she wrote him. So much, she decided, for the promises of politicians. From then on, all promises from Washington to support her projects were taken, as she later put it, "with a very large grain of salt."

In the early thirties, after six years of running her theater, Eva closed it and went to live in the country. Just a month later she was the victim of a disaster. She tried to light a gas furnace that, unknown to her, had a bad leak. There was a huge explosion, and Eva was on fire. She was horribly burned—her flesh hanging in strips from her fingers and arms—and near death. She managed to save her eyes by flinging her hands across them. There seemed little hope that, if she lived, she would not be scarred for life. She made a pain-filled recovery through months of nursing and operations by plastic surgeons to graft skin onto her face and hands. Finally she was ready to appear again in public.

"It was one of the bravest actions in a situation where most of us would have retreated into obscurity," the actor Joseph Schildkraut commented.

Schildkraut also said:

Eva was that marvelously directed personality who was all theatre and yet remained fully human off stage, as most actors are not. She was an advanced woman when the movement was not yet so vocal. She made the best acting version—translations—of Ibsen's plays. Eva knew everything from staging, scenery, painting, to costumes. And most of all how to survive in the tricky wolf world of the theatre, a world dominated, opinionated, by sadistic men who often showed their worst side to a woman.

Although Eva didn't get to our shores until 1915, to me she is always a splendid example of the American woman at her best. This country owes much to her for lifting and refining the values of the stage. And she did it by inspiring so many of us. All without the help of the city or the government. She refused to head the WPA Theatre when it was offered to her, fearing political cant. She was promised, you know, thousands of dollars by the Federal people to help support her ideas in the theatre. But all she got was the brushoff when it came to a final agreement. Poor darling, after she was burned so badly none of us thought she would ever again be on the stage. She fought a fearful fight against disfigurement, with radical surgical grafts, and emerged newborn. Some day the women of America will put up a statue honoring her for what she's done as an inspiration for us.

When Eva came back, she was more talented than ever, and this year (1978) she is still active on stage.

Writing in the first volume of her memoirs, *Dance to the Piper,* Agnes de Mille, another first lady of the stage, presents herself as "an American dancer, a spoiled egocentric wealthy girl, who learned with difficulty to become a worker. . . . My parents were well-educated and fastidious. . . . I was brought up, my mother hoped, a lady, and ladies, my father knew, did not dance."

She was born in 1905 into a famous, even somewhat notorious, family. One grandfather was the well-known political radical Henry George, developer of the "Single Tax" reform plan. Her other grandfather and her father were playwrights, and her mother's side of the family, named Samuel, was Jewish. One uncle was Cecil B. de Mille, the florid film producer of sensual spectaculars.

Her mother and father were born in the Victorian Age, and her mother hardly moved past the Edwardian Age. When her father was called to Hollywood to join his successful brother Cecil in the growing movie industry of the 1920s, Hollywood's foolish, funny golden age of unreason, Agnes lived in the woods of Merrieworld, the summer colony, where she became aware of the deep troubled drama in the lives of her parents and her relatives, and of how much of a woman's life was a façade of good manners and stifled secret passions, an escape into self-made myths.

Agnes was a bright child, given to moods, bemused by nature. At age fourteen she was inspired by a film of Anna Pavlova dancing, and she began to plague her family to allow her to take dancing lessons with a sister who was taking lessons to correct her fallen arches.

Agnes was not built in the image of the perfect dancer; she was neither tall nor slender. But she had the fire and the determination, and she took on the grueling task of years of hard practice. She was to discover that her greatest talent was as a choreographer.

When Agnes finally began her lessons, classic ballet still held sway; tutu-clad little girls pranced on their toes and performed all

Paramount Studios

Agnes de Mille with uncle Cecil B. de Mille in Hollywood.

the steps and turns that were the sacred classics. Agnes, however, knew of a freer world, a world outside that of the accepted theater. She looked even beyond the innovations of Isadora Duncan (1872–1927), who had brought new concepts to the dance world—Isadora's Greek motives improvised to European music were not enough for her. Agnes saw that the freedom of older forms could point to an evolution in the dance. She had grown up in an America that still had memories of frontier shoot outs, dance halls, country hoedowns, cakewalks and the ritual dance and rattle of Indian ceremonies. She thought that there was the basis for a new art in American legends.

Agnes broke into fame when the Ballet Russe de Monte Carlo produced her cowboy-inspired production of *Rodeo,* in which she also danced. It was a landmark in choreography.

This led to *Oklahoma,* a music play whose style changed the whole pattern of that form of entertainment. Agnes then re-created the world of Lizzie Borden in *Fall River Legend.* In *Gentlemen Prefer Blondes* she caught the scene of the 1920s perfectly in her dance forms. Agnes improved the Broadway musical into a near art form, and her more involved productions established firmly her reputation in the ballet world as a respected choreographer with the courage to use American material.

Agnes is a modern woman, aware of the personal tragedies of many women. In early childhood she became aware of the falseness of the picture of marriage inherited from Victorian times, as she watched her parents' life disintegrate, her father turning to flirtations in Hollywood and her mother to living only for the little social tasks that outworn attitudes prescribed for a lady and a wife. Adult reality came to Agnes quickly, and for a long time the dance was her only salvation. A rebel, stubborn and, as she admits, a bit spoiled, she stood among the first of the free women who created in their art forms a position that gave the later women in this movement a foundation and a philosophy.

Agnes de Mille's free life and her work as a choreographer and dance teacher—two professions that were traditionally "men-only" jobs—gave women a new role model to follow. She helped to break the spell of tradition and encouraged other women to work in pivotal careers in the theater. She still remains a student of society, committed to freeing the woman of the naïve world of her childhood. She is able to form and express astute judgments as a woman grown old but still active.

In her choreography Agnes is a realist. Agnes de Mille has freed herself of past myths from other cultures: her cowboy kicks up his heels, her Victorian maiden murders. It amused her to create dance steps for Lorelei's remark about "diamonds are a girl's best friend."

There is no scent of false romance about her work, no Slavic despair or mood. She sees her efforts, which she has called "poignant, precise, honest and utterly distinctive," as very hard work. "This whole business of choreography is hell, *sheer* torture." But she is proud and wise enough to know what she has produced. A former student said:

> De Mille is like a medieval would-be saint who flogs himself with thorn whips and wears a hair shirt. She, too, loves the tools that torture her. And like some saints she has enough ego to know what she has done with her passion—the American dance form has created a woman accepted by all those male dance masters who have really never before accepted a woman as their equal.

Agnes has remained the spiny mistress of progressive, truly American dancing. For her achievements—including the founding of the Agnes de Mille Heritage Dance Theatre—she has been recognized and rewarded many times over. Today she continues to speak out and to write in marvelous prose of her life as a child and as a woman, and of her time and her art.

28.
A Queen Bees Poll

After deciding what personalities I wanted to include in this project, I began a series of surveys, questioning only women, but women of various backgrounds. I explained that I was looking for women who had moved beyond the restraints of their male-oriented society. When they had seen my list, I asked them whom they would have included. The only stipulation I made was that their choices be women not too well known to the public, though they could be women who had once been well known.

One name that came up was that of Imogen Cunningham (1883–1976), a most remarkable genius with the camera. She was born in Oregon and spent a long life of ninety-three years mostly on the West Coast (which may explain why she was so long in coming into international recognition). She attended the University of Washington, where she showed great interest in the mechanics of film studying the early heavy camera as well as platinum printing. She also delved into the complicated chemistry of photography at the Dresden Technical College in Germany. Her earnest dedication to every detail of the art and practice of camera craft made her work known for its clarity and accuracy.

When she returned to Seattle from Germany, she set up her own studio. At first she worked in the romantic soft-focus style of the Impressionist painters. Camera artists of the period were trying to look at the world with the eye of Renoir or Monet, seeking stimulus and sensation rather than reality. The photographer saw himself then as a follower of painting styles instead of an individual in his own right.

Imogen decided that photography was moving in the wrong direction, and she helped change the field by extending the range of photography. Her photographs began to recall the work of Matthew Brady and others. By 1915 she was photographing flowers and images of the living earth with great beauty. She had an acute understanding of nature's forms, and she did not try to make a strip of film into a painted canvas.

Her camera work became her personal signature. She developed into a seeker of faces, a hunter of those who were changing the values of the arts. Her different series of sittings with Edward Weston, Gertrude Stein, Upton Sinclair and Alfred Stieglitz, among others, revealed her ability to move from a leaf to a face and see the relationship of all things as a whole.

Honored at last in old age, in 1967 Imogen Cunningham was elected a fellow of the National Academy of Arts and Sciences.

The most popular modern woman painter in the poll turned out to be Georgia O'Keeffe (b. 1887). She came from a farm in Sun Prairie, Wisconsin, a name almost symbolic of the direct impact of her art. By the age of ten she knew she would be a painter. As she later put it in her crisp, immodest way, "I realized that I had a lot of things in my head that others didn't have. I made up my mind to put down what was in my head."

By 1901 she was studying art at a Madison convent. She went on to the Art Institute of Chicago, and then attended the Art Students League in New York during the days when it was influenced by the Ash Can School of Bellows, Sloan, Shinn, Henri and others. When Georgia was thirty, she suddenly destroyed all her early paintings and drawings and began to work from memory in bold personal patterns. By 1916 she was showing her new style at Alfred Stieglitz's 291 Gallery in New York City.

Eight years later she married Stieglitz, and he continued to exhibit her work until his death. They were a happy and well-matched couple.

She took her themes from various loved places: the Lake George country of still unspoiled Upper New York State, the Rocky Gaspé

Coast of Canada, and the cherished childhood haunts of Wisconsin. Her work grew more patterned and solid as she simplified. When she first saw Taos, New Mexico, in 1929, she knew she had found her colors—the sky and the dry desert, with its white skulls of cattle, the weathered wood, the hard core of mountain flowers that managed to survive. Here mortality and nature stood naked before the Maker.

After the death of her husband, Georgia settled in Abiquiu, New Mexico. She painted, and her stern features so weathered that, in the words of an Elizabethan, one saw "the skull beneath the skin." As she told a reporter, her reason for going into the desert was "because of the earth colors—the ochres and the reds. They are the same colors on my palette." As her work showed, however, it was more than that. It was the nonverbal magic of her forms and the harmony of colors personal to her vision. To her the land became the first days of creation; nothing was overdone, everything was set down with the observant eye of a visionary.

Many honors came to her, and there were numerous retrospective shows. In 1970 the National Institute of Arts and Letters presented her with the Gold Medal for Painting.

A surprising number polled selected Josephine Baker (1902–1975). Not that she was unworthy of being listed—her work with homeless children and her crusades for black causes were reason enough. But for many years, during those expatriate days of transitory pleasures in Paris when the legend of "The Lost Generation" was building, she was known as the nude black dancer (nude but for a string of bananas).

She was born in St. Louis (which she always called St. Louie) and was done with school by the age of eight, when she became a domestic servant to help her family survive ("and *I* did windows"). By the time she was a teenager, she was in vaudeville as a dancer. She had little professional training, but she picked up steps and stage knowledge and stored it away in her slim brown body.

In 1923 the lamentable rage among white visitors for Harlem Negro night life was just beginning, and the Broadway show *Shuffle Along* found Josephine in the chorus line. She advanced quickly, for she had personality and a talent which needed just a little big-city exposure. In 1925 she was in Paris in *La Revue Nègre.* She introduced *Le Jazz Hot* to avid audiences and became "the rage of Paris." She became the headliner of the *Folies Bergère,* and it was here that she did that notorious banana dance. A year later she had her own club, *Chez Josephine,* where she appeared with her sleek black hair ornamented with spit curls, and her lips colored like a sunset. As she grew in fame and fortune, pearls and rare plumes became part of her costumes both off and on stage. Because she knew the value of public advertising, she would often appear on the Champs Elysées leading a pair of leopards on a leash.

Adored by men, she was married four times. Among her husbands were an Italian nobleman, a French flier, and a Jewish band leader. But Josephine's main interest off stage was the homeless children she called "my rainbow tribe." She adopted, fed and housed them by the dozen.

During World War II she remained in France and joined the Underground. She received the *Croix de Guerre* for the dangerous work she did. In 1951, needing money for her adopted children, she toured America, where she was badgered by Walter Winchell as a "communist" as he tried to destroy her reputation and her activities on stage. As usual, she survived.

Misfortune continued to dog her steps. She had enormous debts because of her charity work. She eventually lost her chateau, and there was talk of bankruptcy before she died. But her role in introducing American jazz to Europe makes her one of the great pioneers, and her work with homeless children of all ethnic groups was an innovation in its day.

Another nomination was a woman who was a much more interesting flier than Charles Lindbergh—Jacqueline Cochran. Born in 1910, she fought her way up from an orphanage. At the age of eight, she was working at the looms of a Georgia cotton mill in twelve-hour shifts, her pay six cents an hour. She taught herself to read and write, learned the hairdressing trade, and moved into the world of beauty parlors. After succeeding in that field, she moved on. During a vacation in 1932 she took flying lessons and in three days was soloing. She also studied celestial navigation and learned Morse Code.

Flying exhilarated her, and it became the motivating force of her life. When World War II came, she piloted bombers across the Atlantic to England. In Britain she trained women for the Air Transport Service. She had certain "female" traits that men told stories about. Once when trapped in a burning plane in the air, she wouldn't bail out until she had recovered her handbag and lipstick. On another occasion, after delivering a bomber to England, she refused to be photographed in her flying pants, but changed to a dress for the cameramen.

Her cosmetics firm (whose motto was "Wings of Beauty") saw less and less of her as the war continued. Back in the United States, Jacqueline put together the WASPs, the Women's Airforce Service Pilots. They flew 60 million noncombat miles for the United States Air Force.

When the war was done, she began to devote her attention to breaking speed records. She reached her prime goal in 1964, when she took the women's speed record by flying at 1,429 miles per hour. Very much aware of her abilities, she set a new level of acceptance for women pilots that has since led many other women into the air.

A not surprising nomination in the poll was Virginia Johnson, born in 1925, whose reputation as a scientific sex researcher has made news. But when asked about Johnson and her colleague Dr. William Masters, most women interviewed admitted that they did not know "just *what* the two of them did." Was it something like porno movies? Or, on a clinical level, were they taking the romance out of sex and dehumanizing it? The pair themselves state that they have been "putting sex back into its natural context."

Masters and Johnson have been involved in one of the most serious, deeply researched studies ever done on human sexual patterns and the sexuality of men and women. Virginia aided in the close observation of 700 men and women under actual sexual conditions. Between the two of them they observed over 10,000 sexual encounters, byplays and attitudes—"stuff," as one assistant put it, "that would have shocked the Puritans, enraged Queen Victoria, and baffled the spleenish, morbid Comstock era."

Virginia was not well trained for her vocation. She did not hold a masters certificate in biology or pathology. She had attended a few psychology classes, but had not really learned enough to be called well read. In fact, she had no college degree at all when Masters hired her in 1956. He had just left a gynecological practice that brought in nearly $150,000 a year to turn to sexual research.

Eleven years later, in 1966, she and Masters produced *Human Sexual Response*, a thick book on their studies of human sexuality which not only became a medical bestseller, but also made waves among the general public and did away with many of the myths and legends about sexual behavior.

Together they ran therapy sessions of sexual training based on their research, embarking on new scientific methods. Their programs are said to have helped thousands of couples, married and unmarried, to develop a fuller relationship of sexual freedom and to free themselves from the taboos and fears of the past.

Their work certainly brought the two researchers closer together: Virginia married the doctor in 1971. She noted, "I never quite came of age until I met him."

Masters and Johnson ("Why not Johnson and Masters?" asked one reader) have played a major role in making women equal sexual partners, full personalities no longer dominated by old taboos. Like Virginia Johnson, hundreds of thousands of other women also "came of age" as a result of the work of this woman and this man.

There can be no summing up of the Queen Bees of today, for we are still too close to their achievements and to their contemporaries' resentment of their works. However, there are certain individuals I would like to add to the list of potential future candidates.

Karen Horney insists it is the culture rather than the anatomy we should think about in evaluating modern women. Ms. Horney, a keen analyst, says, "It is our culture that forces women and men to act differently." She feels that nearly all psychological ideas and theories are slanted to favor men and that women have often too easily accepted men's ideas of them. Her ardent sponsoring of such thoughts got her fired from her job as training analyst for the New York Psychoanalytic Society.

In protest of Ms. Horney's dismissal, a number of members of the Society left and formed the American Institute for the Advancement of Psychoanalysis. Among them was Clara M. Thompson. In an essay on "The Role of Women in This Culture" (1941) she wrote:

> In this country today women occupy a unique position. They are probably freer to live their own lives than in any patriarchal country in the world. This does not mean that they have ceased to be an underprivileged group. They are discriminated against in many situations without regard for their needs or ability. One would expect, therefore, to find the reality situation bringing out inferiority feelings not only because of a reaction to the immediate situation but because of family teaching in childhood based on the same cultural attitude.

Following is a list of some outstanding twentieth-century women who have certainly managed to rise above the adverse cultural influences deplored by Ms. Horney and Ms. Thompson.

Mary McLeod (1875–1955) was a black woman who, against great odds, became an educator and administrator and opened a pioneer school for black children in Florida in 1904. Today the school is known as the Bethune-Cookman Institute. President Roosevelt appointed Mary McLeod as a special assistant for minority affairs, and she helped draft the United Nations charter.

There are writers who produced valuable literary innovations, like Amy Lowell (1874–1925), one of the founders of the Imagist school of poetry, and Carson McCullers (1917–1967), whose novels rivaled those of William Faulkner in revealing the inner secrets of the southern mystique. Nor can one overlook Edna St. Vincent Millay (1892–1950), whose poetry combined vigor and quality with the voice of protest.

And Margaret Bourke-White (1906–1971), the fearless photographer, showed the world that danger and skill in covering world events was not only a man's job.

Certainly Wall Street and investment specialists must admit that Sylvia Porter (b. 1913) writes one of the finest financial advice columns. But at first she had to sign herself S. F. Porter so readers *might* assume she was a man.

Racial bigotry was fought by Marian Anderson (b. 1902), of whom Toscanini said, "A voice such as one hears once in a hundred years." Yet in 1939 this black singer was refused the use of Constitution Hall by the Daughters of the American Revolution. Later, aided by Eleanor Roosevelt (who resigned from the DAR), Marian Anderson arranged a concert at the Lincoln Memorial which over 75,000 people attended.

Ella Fitzgerald (b. 1918) rose above her orphanage upbringing to do much to bring jazz forward as an original American art form.

Irene Castle (1894–1969) and her husband Vernon revived ballroom dancing: "We made dancing look like the fun it was."

Other women performed on a different stage. There was the remarkable and wild Isadora Duncan (1878–1927), who has been called "the Sarah Bernhardt of the dance." Modern before her time, she freed serious dancing from classical ballet. Katherine Dunham (b. 1912) added the patterns of tribal dances to her work. Martha Graham (b. 1894) led the avant-garde dance into social protest by mixing disturbing modern Freudian themes with folk traditions. She said, "I'd rather have people against me than indifferent."

There was Rachel Carson (1907–1965), whose *Silent Spring* brought a clear warning of the dangers of polluting the environment by calling attention to the devastating damage being done by pesticides. Now we are all aware of this, but she dared to speak out loudly when few would listen.

Mother Frances Xavier Cabrini (1850–1917) was the first American citizen to be officially made a saint. And although her motives have been questioned, gospel preacher Aimee Semple McPherson (1890–1944) inspired hundreds of thousands to believe in her and in God.

For a long time, the success of women in sports has not been looked upon as freakish. In 1926 Gertrude Ederle (b. 1906) became the first woman to swim the English Channel, accomplishing the feat in just over fourteen hours, and "Babe" Mildred Didrickson (1914–1956) was called "without question the athletic phenomenon of all time, man *or* woman."

Many women have contributed to the political world. Congresswoman Jeannette Rankin (1881–1973) voted against entering the war in 1917, and again in 1941. Eleanor Roosevelt is an obvious example, even though she never held elected office. Bella Abzug (b. 1920) has fought the men who would push women aside in politics. She admits that some think her "impatient, impetuous, uppity, rude, profane, brash, overbearing . . . but I *am* a very serious woman." Another very serious woman is Shirley Chisholm (b. 1924), a black congresswoman who announced for the presidency at the Democratic Convention of 1972 and got 152 votes.

The list could go on with more of those who changed society and the role of its women.

But the cause is far from won. Many women still feel bound by old restraints and societal views. Emma Jung, in an essay "On the Nature of the Animus" (1931), quotes a female patient's reaction to the painting *Urgo, the Magic Dragon:*

> *A snake or dragon-like creature was represented in the picture together with a girl who was under his power. The dragon had the ability to stretch out in all directions so that there was no possibility for the girl to evade his reach; at any movement of hers he could extend himself on that side and make escape impossible.*

The strength of that dragon is still awesome. Men still dominate business, the arts and sports. Inroads have been made, but the bias against women cannot easily be removed, for it has existed since the Christian saints first raged against women as objects of filth and lust, and has been reinforced by the domination of the coercive Victorian husband over the body, soul and wealth of his wife and daughters. Even in relatively modern fiction we find "sexual sinners" such as Anna Karenina and Madame Bovary resolving their fate through suicide.

Margaret Mead might have been right in thinking that no matter how wise the man, he often hinders as much as he helps in placing women in their proper place as an equal. She wrote of Freud's contributions in an essay called "On Freud's View of Female Psychology" (1933): "It is a pity that he understood women so little . . . he was . . . completely culture-bound."

Perhaps that bitter critic of existence Jonathan Swift best summed up the whole world of the Queen Bees when he wrote: "The bee . . . does the whole business of life at once, and at the same time feeds, and works, and diverts itself."

And Gloria Steinem notes, "I feel an odd mixture of elation and celebration that we have grown . . . and seriousness sometimes bordering on despair at how far we have to go."

List of Sources
and
Acknowledgments

Much that went into this text was from private journals, letters and items from period newspapers and magazines. Numerous other volumes, some long out of print, were checked for dates, data and detail. Following are those that were most helpful:

Abbott, Lyman, *Henry Ward Beecher,* 1903

Adams, Grace, *The Mad Forties,* 1942

Adams, Henry, *Education of Henry Adams,* 1918

Addams, Jane, *Twenty Years at Hull House,* 1924

Allen, Frederick Lewis, *Only Yesterday,* 1957

Amory, Cleveland, *Who Killed Society,* 1903

Anburey, Thomas, *Travels Through the Interior Parts of America,* 1789, 1976

Anderson, Margaret, *My Thirty Years' War,* 1930

Aquinas, Thomas, *Summa Theologica* (selection), 1920

Aretz, Gertrude, *The Elegant Women,* 1932

Auchincloss, Louis, *Edith Wharton,* 1971

Baldwin, Charles D., *Stanford White,* 1931

Barney, Natalie Clifford, *Traits et Portraits,* 1963

Beach, Sylvia, *Shakespeare & Co.,* 1956

Beard, Mary, *America Through Women's Eyes,* 1933

Bebel, A., *Women Under Socialism,* 1923

Beebe, Lucius, *The Big Spenders,* 1966

Beecher, Henry Ward, *Lectures to a Young Man,* 1860

Beer, Thomas, *The Mauve Decade,* 1926

Benson, Mary, *Women in the Eighteenth Century,* 1935

Birmingham, Stephen, *Our Crowd,* 1967

Blackwell, Alice Stone, *Lucy Stone,* 1930

Brinnin, John Malcolm, *The Third Rose,* 1959

Burt, Nathaniel, *The Perennial Philadelphians,* 1963

Butterfield, Roger, *The American Past,* 1957

Churchill, Allen, *The Improper Bohemians,* 1959

Churchill, Allen, *The Splendor Seekers,* 1974

Cohen, David L., *The Good Old Days,* 1940

Comstock, Anthony, *Traps for the Young,* 1883

Crockett, Albert Steven, *Peacocks on Parade,* 1931

Crosby, Caresse, *The Passionate Years,* 1953

Crouse, Russell, *It Seems Like Yesterday,* 1939

Crowninshield, Francis, *Manners for the Metropolis,* 1908

Day, Charles, *Etiquette with a Glance at Bad Habits,* 1846

de Tocqueville, Alexis, *Democracy in America,* 1838

De Wolfe, Elsie, *The House in Good Taste,* 1913

Dickens, Charles, *American Notes,* ND

Dictionary of American Biography, ND

Dingwall, Eric, *The American Woman,* 1957

Duncan, Isadore, *My Life,* 1927, 1953

Eliot, Elizabeth, *Heiresses & Coronets,* 1959

Eller, Elizabeth, *Queens of American Society,* 1867

Ellis, Havelock, *Studies in the Psychology of Sex,* 1911

Fabian, Warner, *Flaming Youth,* 1934

Flanner, Janet, *An American in Paris,* 1940

Furness, Clifton, *The Genteel Female,* 1931

Goldman, Emma, *Living My Life,* 1931

Gurnas, J. C., *Great Times,* 1974

Hall, Captain Basil, *Travels in North America,* 1825

Handler, Oscar, *This Was America,* 1949

Hartley, Florence, *The Ladies' Book of Etiquette,* 1872

Herold, J. C., *Mistress to an Age,* 1958

Hicks, Granville, *John Reed,* 1936

Hoge, Alice, *Cissie Patterson,* 1966

Hoyt, Edwin, *The Vanderbilts & Their Fortunes,* 1962

Hoyt, Edwin, *The Whitneys,* 1976

Janeway, Elizabeth, *Man's World, Woman's Place,* 1972

Jensen, Oliver, *The Revolt of American Women,* 1952

Johnston, Johanna, *Mrs. Satan,* 1967

Jones, Ernest, *Life & Times of Sigmund Freud,* 1955

Kavaler, Lucy, *The Astors,* 1966

Kellogg, Grace, *The Two Lives of Edith Wharton,* 1965

Keyserling, Herman, *America Set Free,* 1930

Koch, Robert, *Louis C. Tiffany,* 1964

Leighton, Isabel, ed., *The Aspirin Age,* 1949, 1968

Levin, Phyllis, *The Wheels of Fashion,* 1965

Lewis, Arthur H., *The Day They Shook the Plum Tree,* 1963

Lewis, R. B., *Edith Wharton,* 1975

Lochner, Louis, *America's Don Quixote, Henry Ford,* 1924

Longstreet, Abby, *Social Etiquette of New York,* 1875

Longstreet, Stephen, *Chicago: 1860–1919,* 1973

Longstreet, Stephen, *City on Two Rivers,* 1975

Longworth, Alice, *Crowded Hours,* 1933

Luhan, Mabel Dodge, *Movers and Shakers,* 1936

Lutz, Alma, *Susan B. Anthony,* 1959

Lynes, Russell, *The Domesticated Americans,* 1963

Lynes, Russell, *The Tastemakers,* 1949

McAllister, Ward, *Society as I Have Known It,* 1891

McCabe, James D., Jr., *Lights & Shadows of New York Life,* 1872

McLean, Evalyn Walsh, and Sparkes, Boyden, *Father Struck It Rich,* 1936, 1975

Manners, Ande, *Poor Cousins,* 1972

Martin, Frederick Townsend, *The Passing of the Idle Rich,* 1911, 1975

Martineau, Harriet, *Society in America,* 1942

Maurois, André Lebic, *George Sand,* 1953

Mead, Margaret, *Male and Female,* 1950

Miller, Rosalind S., *Gertrude Stein: Form & Intelligibility,* 1949

Millett, Kate, *Sexual Politics,* 1970

Montagu, Ashley, *Sex, Man and Society,* 1968

Morris, Lloyd, *Not So Long Ago,* 1949

Mumford, Lewis, *The Brown Decade,* 1931

O'Connor, Harvey, *The Astors,* 1941

O'Connor, Harvey, *The Guggenheims,* 1937

O'Higgins, Patrick, *Madame,* 1971

Packard, Vance, *The Sexual Wilderness,* 1968

Post, Emily, *Etiquette, The Blue Book of Social Usage,* 1957

Pulitzer, Ralph, *New York Society on Parade,* 1920

Riis, Jacob, *How the Other Half Lives,* 1890

Rogers, Agnes, *Women Are Here to Stay,* 1949

Ross, Isabel, *Ladies of the Press,* 1936

Ross, Isabel, *Taste in America,* 1967

Saarinen, Aline, *The Proud Possessors,* 1958

Sachs, Emanie, *The Terrible Siren,* 1928

Shannon, William V., *The American Irish,* 1963

Shaplen, Robert, *Free Love and Heavenly Sinners,* 1954

Shattuck, Roger, *The Banquet Years,* 1955

Sigourney, Lydia, *Letters to Young Ladies,* 1859

Simon, Linda, *The Biography of Alice B. Toklas,* 1977

Sinclair, Arthur, *Emancipation of the American Woman,* 1966

Smith, Matthew, *Sunshine and Shadow in New York,* 1868

Smith, Page, *Daughters of the Promised Land,* 1970

Sparkes, Boyden, and Moore, Samuel, *Hetty Green,* 1930

Sprigge, Elizabeth, *Gertrude Stein,* 1957

Stein, Gertrude, *Autobiography of Alice B. Toklas,* 1933

Stein, Leon, *The Triangle Fire,* 1962

Stevenson, Elizabeth, *Babbitts & Bohemians,* 1967

Stowe, Lyman Beecher, *Saints, Sinners and Beechers,* 1934

Stric, Anne, *Injustice for All,* 1977

Sullivan, Mark, *Our Times,* 1900–1925, 6 vols., 1935

Swanberg, W. A., *Luce,* 1972

Tarbell, Ida, *All in the Day's Work,* 1935

Thomson, Virgil, *Virgil Thomson,* 1966

Toklas, Alice B., *The Alice B. Toklas Cook Book,* 1954

Toklas, Alice B., *What Is Remembered,* 1963

Trollope, Anthony, *North America,* 1863

Trollope, Frances, *The Domestic Manners of the Americans,* 1832

Untermeyer, Louis, *Makers of the Modern World,* 1955

Vanderbilt, Cornelius, Jr., *Queen of the Golden Age,* 1952

Van Every, Edward, *Sins of New York,* 1933

Van Vechten, Carl, *Parties,* 1930

Veblen, Thorstein, *The Theory of the Leisure Class,* 1889

Ware, Caroline F., *Greenwich Village,* 1920–1930, 1935

Wecter, Dixon, *The Saga of American Society,* 1937

Wells, Evelyn, *Champagne Days of San Francisco,* 1947

Wells, H. G., *The Future of America,* 1906

Wertheimer, Barbara M., *We Were There,* 1977

Wharton, Edith, *The Age of Innocence,* 1920

Wharton, Edith, *A Backward Glance,* 1934

Wilson, Edmund, *The American Earthquake,* 1958

Woodward, W. E., *The Way Our People Lived,* 1944

Wylie, Philip, *Generation of Vipers,* 1942

Zangwell, Israel, *The Melting Pot,* 1909

Index